Faithful Witnesses
Leader's Guide

Faithful Witnesses

Leader's Guide

Richard Stoll Armstrong

The Geneva Press
Philadelphia

Scripture quotations from the Revised Standard Version of the Bible are copyrighted 1946, 1952, © 1971, 1973 by the Division of Christian Education of the National Council of the Churches of Christ in the U.S.A. and are used by permission.

Excerpts appearing in this publication from the following books are included by permission of the publisher, The Westminster Press: *Service Evangelism* by Richard Stoll Armstrong, copyright © 1979 The Westminster Press; *The Pastor as Evangelist* by Richard Stoll Armstrong, copyright © 1984 Richard Stoll Armstrong.

Book design by Gene Harris

First edition

Published by The Geneva Press®
Philadelphia, Pennsylvania

PRINTED IN THE UNITED STATES OF AMERICA
9 8 7 6 5 4 3 2

Library of Congress Cataloging-in-Publication Data

Armstrong, Richard Stoll, 1924–
    Faithful witnesses.   Leader's guide.

    Bibliography: p.
    1. Evangelistic work.   2. Witness bearing
(Christianity)   3. Presbyterian Church (U.S.A.)—
Membership.   4. Presbyterian Church—United States—
Membership.   I. Title.
BV3790.A726   1987   248'.5   87-23661
ISBN 0-664-24076-3 (pbk.)

*This book is dedicated to the memory of
B. Kong Han, 1921–1987,
a faithful witness who did not live to see
the completion of this project,
to which he gave inspired leadership.*

Contents

Preparing
for the Course

There are two parts to the Presbyterian Evangelism Course. The first consists of twelve weekly class sessions of approximately two hours each.* The second part is a supervised calling experience of two and a half hours a week for four weeks. The purpose of the calling experience is to provide a structured opportunity for the participants to reinforce and apply the learning that has taken place in class and to develop evangelistic calling skills through on-the-job training.

Recruiting the Participants

"God wants you!" In the recruitment of participants for the Presbyterian Evangelism Course to be held in your church, some people may respond to public announcements, but personal invitations are better, either from you or from someone who has been assigned that responsibility. Those asked should be presented with the challenge of a 34-hour commitment; if there are those who are willing to make such a commitment of time and effort, your church will have a group of persons who have been trained for an effective and ongoing ministry of evangelism.

---

*In order to adapt to local circumstances, these sessions may be scheduled over a shorter period of time, but it is important to cover all the material, including the home assignments.

"Any number can play!" The course can be presented to any number of participants, limited only by the difficulty of handling groups of more than a certain number. Thirty people is an ideal upper limit. If there are only one or two recruits, consider having them attend a course conducted by or in cooperation with another church or group of churches.

"Put it in writing!" Send a follow-up letter to those who agree to come, expressing joy about their acceptance, reiterating the purpose of the course, containing needed information (dates, time and place, what, when, and where to pay, what to bring, how to dress, and what to do in preparation), enclosing an agenda, and reminding them to pray for and about the course. With groups of ten or more, it's a good idea to send a second letter enclosing a list of the participants as soon as the registration is complete.

"Think about it!" Ask those who sign up to think about and put down answers to the following questions:

1. What is evangelism? Write your own definition, as you now understand it.
2. Do you have any personal fears or concerns about evangelism? If so, what are they?
3. What are your personal hopes for this course? What would make it a really worthwhile experience for you?

"All or nothing!" If someone knows she or he cannot attend the entire course from start to finish, it would be better for that person to wait for another time. There should be no part-time participants, no "in-again-out-again Finnegans."

"Now hear this!" Although the participants are invited individually, posters, notices in the Sunday bulletin, articles in the church newsletter, and announcements from the pulpit will keep the congregation informed, stimulate interest, and turn up potential candidates for the next time the course is offered. Keep a list of those you want to invite at some future date.

Registration Fee (Optional)

Some churches charge a registration fee to help defray the cost of materials, refreshments, and other items. It is up to the particular church to determine the appropriate amount, if any, being careful not to exclude anyone who may not be able to afford the fee.

Gearing Up for Your Classes

Physical Facilities

Room size. The room should be large enough for all the participants to meet together as a group (preferably in a circle, or in a semicircle for very large groups), with sets of four folding chairs (or five, if there are more than twenty-four participants) arranged around the periphery of the room for small-group exercises. (Some role-play exercises will require different groupings.) All class activities throughout the course—with the possible exception of meals, if your schedule calls for any—can be in the same room. There should be plenty of wall space for posting newsprint sheets.

Chairs. Comfortable chairs are best for the main circle, while folding chairs are better for the small-group exercises; they are more easily moved and take up less room. Arrange the chairs in each small group in a circle, as close together as possible, and keep the circles as far apart as space allows.

Tables. Folding tables may be an asset with smaller numbers of participants but are not a necessity. Although they facilitate note-taking and writing on loose sheets of newsprint, they occupy space and prevent closeness when the larger group gathers. People will have their workbooks for note-taking.

Lighting. The ideal situation is to have enough table lamps or standing lamps to provide adequate lighting for each small group and the main circle of chairs. Overhead lighting will do, if it isn't too glaring. Try to create a comfortable rather than formal classroom atmosphere. If that is impossible, go with what you have, but make sure there is enough light for people of all ages to be able to read and write.

Materials and Equipment

Marking pens. Wide-tip felt pens of various colors are a necessity. Make sure they are not dried up. Keep an ample supply on hand, with a fresh pen for each group according to their color code (if used). Use different-colored pens as you write, to punctuate graphically things you have said along the way. These sheets can then be put up on the wall as a visible and decorative summary of what the group is learning. You can make your signs or charts while the participants are doing their small-group exercises.

Newsprint. A large-size pad of newsprint (the bigger the better) is indispensable. Separate sheets of newsprint will be used for some small-group exercises. As a safety precaution, use a second sheet to protect the surface beneath from being stained by the felt-tip pens.

Easel. A sturdy easel that permits easy removal of the news-print sheets and has a built-on tray or ledge for pens is another must. You will be using these items throughout the course.

Masking tape. Have half-inch masking tape handy for use in attaching newsprint sheets and color-code signs. Masking tape tears off the roll easily and does not harm the surface to which it is attached.

Name tags. There are three main reasons for using name tags. The first and most obvious one is for identification. Second, they are an invaluable aid to group building for any course in which the participants are not likely to know one another. Third, name tags can be used to facilitate the movement of participants into small groups and to assign roles in small-group exercises and role-playing. Write the names in letters big and bold enough to be read by everyone in the circle. Plain white name tags that allow plenty of room for writing (and for color coding, if used), that are easily attached, and that are sturdy enough to last as long as they are needed are best. Prepare the tags ahead and arrange them alphabetically for the participants to pick up as they arrive. *Be sure to collect the name tags at the end of each class.*

Note: If there are fifteen or more participants, try a color-coding system. Work out your coding in advance according to the number of participants, so that they are assigned to different groups for different exercises. Some of the exercises will be done in pairs, some in threes, and some in groups of four or five. Attach large colored dots to the wall near each small-group circle. This enables you to say, "Go to the circle that matches dot number two on your name tag." There they will find the other persons who have been assigned by you to be with them in that exercise. This process eliminates confusion and saves an immense amount of time, when you are working with larger groups. There is an explanation and rotation chart on pp. 127 and 131 of *Service Evangelism.*

Piano. If there is a piano (or guitar) and someone to play it, you can use it to accompany the singing during your devotional times and to liven up the break periods.

Participants' books. Each participant will receive a workbook at the start of the course. It will serve as both a notebook for the course and a textbook for ongoing use and should be brought to each class session. Be sure to keep a workbook for yourself.

Handouts. Handouts will include some song sheets, which you will want to prepare for use in the devotionals, a list of the participants for each enrollee, and blank paper as needed.

Tearouts. Tearout sheets at the back of the workbook comprise three Benchmarks and a final evaluation sheet, to be completed and handed in at the appropriate times, according to the instructions in this guide.

Other needs. Have extra Bibles on hand for those who forget to bring theirs, and a supply of sharpened pencils. For those who are not familiar with the hymns suggested for the openings and closings—identified by number and the initials *HB* (*Hymnbook*), *HL* (*Hymnal*), or *WB* (*Worshipbook*), you may want to provide hymn books.

Refreshments

The participants will appreciate your having coffee, tea, cocoa, or juice available, with an ample supply of cookies, crackers, or other snacks, during the registration period and break times.

Leadership Style

This guide provides the structure and content for the course, but not the leadership. As leader, you must be familiar with the material, but you need not be rigidly bound to it. Some of the text is directed to you and should be absorbed and digested before it is taught. Other parts are intended to be communicated directly to the class, with occasional suggestions as to how the ideas might be worded.

Each leader weaves his or her own personality and style into the material. The concepts are explained; it is up to you to put them into words the class can understand. Use illustrations that communicate and language with which you and they are comfortable. Relate the exercises and role plays to the participants' experience.

The form and content of the course call for a dialogical style of leadership, one that recognizes and affirms the knowledge, experience, and insights of the participants. It is not intended to be a passive learning experience for the members of the class; the format calls for their active participation throughout the course, with many exercises and much discussion, among class members as a whole as well as in small groups. There will be many occasions, however, when you will need to *be* the leader, such as when you are introducing a new topic or theme, explaining a concept, giving directions, or answering questions.

It is hoped that important by-products of the course will be an increased sense of self-worth and a mutual appreciation and respect on the part of all involved, to the end that each one may become a more confident and competent faith communicator, helping one another to be faithful witnesses.

Time Allotments

The time allotments indicated after each section heading for the various class activities are only approximations to guide you in your teaching. The first number indicates the time allotted for that part; the number in parentheses is the total time elapsed. If you use less time than is suggested for a particular exercise, that's fine; you can always use the extra time elsewhere. If you spend more time than is specified for one part, you will have to make adjustments somewhere else in order to stay within the two hours set aside for each session. Or you and the class may decide to continue for slightly more than two hours, in order to cover all the material in a particular session. What is required is disciplined leadership, flexible enough to bend the time schedule but not to break it. If you stick fairly close to the suggested times for the various activities, you will be able to cover all the material in twelve weeks. If you wish to extend the course for a week or two, that is entirely up to you and the participants.

Home Assignments

Home assignments are listed at the end of each session in the workbook. Make sure the participants are doing the assignments each week, but try not to be tempted into spending too much time discussing them during class. Instead, encourage the participants to talk about the assignments with one another outside the classroom. That will further extend and reinforce the learning experience.

Prayer

Undergirding all the preparations should be the prayers of the congregation, the participants, and the leader—you! Ask the prayer circles, if there are such, to make the course and the participants the subject of their special intercessory prayers. In whatever media are used to publicize the course, encourage the continued prayers of the congregation. To paraphrase a familiar text, "Unless the Lord watches over the course, they labor in vain who teach it!"

WEEK ONE

Getting Started

Registration

Tell participants to arrive 15 minutes early on the first day, for registration. Make sure that the room is properly set up, with the necessary materials and equipment on hand, refreshments ready, and the registration table prepared, with name tags arranged alphabetically, a workbook for each person (including yourself), and someone to register the participants and collect any fees owed. These formalities can be greatly simplified if there are only a handful of people involved. Name tags, for example, may not be necessary.

As the participants arrive, greet them cordially, give them their name tags, and invite them to have some refreshments while they introduce themselves to one another. By circulating among them, you will facilitate the getting-acquainted process.

Welcome and Opening Devotions   *10 (10)*

At the appointed time, ask the participants to be seated in the center circle of chairs (or semicircle if there is a large group). When all are comfortably settled, welcome them officially, tell them where the rest rooms and other facilities are, state the general purpose of the course, and give out the workbooks; each person will be using a book throughout the course for taking notes and doing the exercises and also as a textbook. Having dealt with any questions that arise, you are ready to begin with a brief devotional exercise. (There are twelve of these, grouped at the back of the workbook.) Distribute the song sheets at this time and ask the participants to insert them in their workbooks for future use. You may want to ask for volunteers from the group to lead these exercises.

Getting Acquainted   *30 (40)*

There are many ways of breaking the ice. If you have an ice-breaker with which you are familiar and comfortable, use it. One way of getting acquainted is to start with yourself and then go around the circle, asking people to introduce themselves and mention something interesting they have done recently or give some interesting fact about themselves that most of the group would not know. When everyone has spoken, ask how many have always been Presbyterians and how many ever belonged to some other church. What denominations? If the group is fairly large, other denominations undoubtedly will be represented in the backgrounds of several of those present, in which case you can comment on their ecumenical makeup and commend them for being such an interesting group (they always are!). If the group is not too large and you have not used up the thirty minutes allotted to this activity, you could ask, "Who can tell us something interesting about so-and-so?" It is beautiful to see the way they affirm one another, and it brings them close together in a hurry.

Sharing Hopes   *20 (1:00)*

EXERCISE 1: My Personal Hopes for This Course

Divide into as many groups of four as possible. (If there are only six persons, have two groups of three.) Ask the groups to turn to Exercise 1 in the workbook and follow the instructions, beginning with the question, "What do I hope will happen to me as a result of my involvement in this course?" As they share their hopes, each group should develop a composite list and record the hopes on newsprint.

Discussion. Everyone then regathers in the center circle, and the recorder from each small group reads the list. As each group reports, you can develop an overall list of hopes for the entire class, including an idea only once and putting check marks by it for the repeats.

Ten-minute Break *10 (1:10)*

If everybody doesn't know everybody else, suggest that during the break they seek out and chat with someone they didn't know well, if at all, before they arrived. While they're visiting with one another, you have time to put up your composite list of hopes on a highly visible part of the wall. The small-group lists can be hung near the corresponding groups of chairs.

Thoughts About Evangelism   *30 (1:40)*

EXERCISE 2: My Present Thoughts About Evangelism

At the end of the break redivide the class into *different* small groups of four (using the color code, if that is helpful). Ask them to turn to Exercise 2 in the workbook and explain that this will provide an opportunity to share their thoughts about evangelism. It is to be hoped that many of them will have been thinking ahead about this, but give them a few minutes to write down their definitions and concerns if they have not already done so. Signal when it is time to start sharing with the others in their small group. After twenty minutes, regather in the main circle.

Discussion. Invite the groups to read the definitions they selected. Then ask them to share their lists of concerns. Again, you may want to develop an overall list for the class. During the reporting you might offer brief comments that you feel are pertinent, in order to identify significant points or findings.

Defining Our Terms   *15 (1:55)*

Definitions of Evangelism

Call attention to the New Age Dawning definition of evangelism in the workbook, as well as to the other definitions. The definitions will be read as part of the home assignment for next week.

Mini-Definitions of Some Related Terms

After regathering in the center circle, begin as follows: "Turn to the Mini-Definitions in your workbook. Here are a number of key terms we shall be using in the course. Let's take a few minutes to run through the list to see if there are questions about any of the definitions. The purpose at this point is for clarification only; this is not the time to discuss all the implications of these terms. We simply want to define them, so that everyone will know how the words are being used." Go down through the list.

Closing   5 *(2:00)*

Thank the class for their participation and remind them of the home assignment for the next session. Stress the importance of their blocking out some time to do the assignments each week. Then have them stand and join hands in a circle, and invite them to share words or phrases that express their feelings at this point. When the sharing subsides, close with a brief prayer. Remind everyone of the next meeting time, and dismiss them with a benediction.

WEEK TWO

Making
the Case

Opening Devotions 5 (5)

Choose one of the devotions at the back of the workbook or plan your own. A simple service could include singing a couple of hymns, having someone read an appropriate scripture passage, and asking someone else to offer a prayer.

Review 15 (20)

Display the newsprint sheets from last week in a prominent place on the wall. Mention briefly what was covered in the first class session: "We got acquainted, we shared our hopes for the course, and we began our discussion of evangelism. Any comments? Questions? Thoughts? Feelings?" This dialogue provides an early benchmark to give you a sense of where the participants are at this point in the learning process.

Next, call attention again to the mini-definitions in the workbook and ask the participants if they would like to add any relevant terms. Can anyone suggest simple definitions for any new terms mentioned? If you yourself need time to come up with a good mini-definition, say so. If there are no new terms, point out that they may want to add terms now and then, as they encounter them in the course.

Now look at the goals for this session, as listed under Week 2 in the workbook. Have someone read them aloud.

The Biblical Mandate
for Evangelism

Ask if there are any questions or comments about the article they read at home, entitled "Faithful Witnesses." Take a few minutes, if necessary, to deal with questions that arise. If there are none, you are ready for the next exercise.

Motivating People for Evangelism   *30 (50)*

EXERCISE 3: The Motivation for Evangelism

Divide into groups of four (use color coding, if helpful). Ask the class to turn to Exercise 3 and follow the instructions. Tell them they will have five minutes for each question and that you will give them a signal when it is time to move on to the next part of the exercise.

Discussion. After twenty minutes reassemble in the main circle and have the small groups report. First ask if they thought of any other biblical texts for evangelism. Then ask what ideas they came up with for motivating people to do evangelism. Put their newsprint sheets on the wall.

Stating Some Premises   *10 (1:00)*

One helpful response to the problem of motivation is the liberating concept that evangelism is a ministry of the whole church and not the exclusive province of a few charismatic individuals. The nature of the church's evangelistic ministry is described in the article "Faithful Witnesses." For those who would like to do further reading on this topic, see *The Church as Evangelist* by George Sweazey (Harper & Row, 1978) and *Service Evangelism* by Richard Stoll Armstrong (Westminster Press, 1979).

Not everyone is gifted as a preacher or a "soul-winner" or is comfortable ringing doorbells for Christ, but there is something every church member can do to help the *church* fulfill its ministry of evangelism. Ask the class to turn to "Operating Premises for the Church as Evangelist." Read them aloud one at a time, stopping after each one to ask the class if there are any questions. These are the assumptions on which rests the church's corporate ministry of evangelism and the claim that there is something every church member can do to help the church fulfill that ministry.

Five-minute Break 5 *(1:05)*

Helping the Church to Be the Evangelist

EXERCISE 4: What *Every* Church Member Can Do 25 *(1:30)*

Divide the class into groups of four. Ask them to turn to "What Every Church Member Can Do to Help the Church Evangelize" and list everything they can think of in five minutes. ("Simply list them; don't elaborate.") When the time is up, ask them to share what they have written with the other members of their small group, listing each new idea on newsprint.

Discussion. Regather in the large circle and ask the small groups to share their composite lists. You may want to compile an overall list for the class, eliminating duplications. When all their ideas have been listed, turn to "A Personal Covenant" on page 97 of the workbook. Run through the list quickly, inviting the class to suggest briefly how each activity helps the church evangelize. The fuller the church pews on Sunday, for example, the more positive the impact on visitors and members alike. The connection of each activity to evangelism is fairly obvious. Suggest that they give thought to how many of the items they would be willing to covenant to do.

EXERCISE 5: What *Some* Church Members Can Do 25 *(1:55)*

"Remembering Paul's teachings about the interdependence of the members of the body of Christ, all contributing to the unity, welfare, and ministry of the whole, what are the kinds of things some church members can do that other members may not be able to do to help the church evangelize?"

Ask the class to turn to Exercise 5, and divide into groups of four. Supply each group with newsprint and felt-tip pens (matching their respective group colors on the wall, if color coding is used). They are to brainstorm all the ways they can think of to help the church evangelize. Prime the pump by suggesting two or three ways to begin with, such as singing in a choir, teaching a church school class, participating in a youth fellowship or a singles group, or providing transportation to church for someone who needs it. Ask each group to appoint a recorder.

Discussion. Regather in the center circle. Ask the recorders to report briefly; each succeeding recorder should add only *new* ideas (not mentioned by previous groups) or underscore repetitions. Put the newsprint sheets on the wall in a highly visible place. Do not elaborate, but affirm and enthuse as appropriate. After all the teams have reported, have the class turn to "The Church as Evangelist" on page 95 of the workbook. The suggestions should be categorized, with many blank places provided for the participants to add ideas gained from this exercise and discussion.

Closing   5 (2:00)

"We have been thinking about ways we can help the church fulfill its ministry of evangelism. Does anyone have any final comments or thoughts to share, before we have our closing prayer?" After leaving time to respond, say, "We have been talking about the church, which we have learned is not the kingdom of God but is a manifestation, an expression, of the kingdom. Let's stand now and sing together 'I Love Thy Kingdom, Lord'" (*HB* 435 or *HL* 337; or include this hymn among the song sheets). After the hymn, offer a brief closing prayer. Remind them of the assignment for next time and dismiss them with a benediction.

WEEK THREE

Overcoming the Barriers

Opening Devotions   *10 (10)*

Review   *10 (20)*

Place the composite lists of "The Church as Evangelist" on the wall where they are easily seen. You might begin by saying something to this effect: "Last week we discussed the biblical mandate for evangelism and shared our ideas about motivating people for evangelism. We saw that the church is the evangelist, and we listed ways that every church member can help the church fulfill its evangelistic ministry. We also listed things that some people can do, which others may not be able to do. Now we are going to talk about interpersonal evangelism and the importance of listening." The objectives for this third session are listed in the workbook. Have someone read them aloud.

Call attention to the fact that one of the things they listed which *some* church members can do to help the church evangelize is "witnessing," or "sharing my faith with others." (If it wasn't listed, add it!) Then ask, "How many of you feel that you could use some help in this regard?" Most people will readily admit they could use some help.

Barriers to Interpersonal Evangelism (Witnessing)

EXERCISE 6: Barriers to Witnessing   *25 (45)*

Divide the class into threes and ask them to turn to "Barriers to Witnessing" and the list of personal barriers. Give a brief word of instruction. "Put a check mark by each barrier that you feel applies to you. Add any others you can think of." After five minutes, ask them to share their list with the other two persons in their group. After five more minutes, say, "Did you add any other barriers to the list?" Then ask them to write in the space provided what they can do to overcome their personal barriers. After five more minutes, ask them to share within their groups what they have written. "Have you any suggestions for one another?"

Discussion. Without regathering, ask how it went. Get a few comments from the different groups (no in-depth discussion). Explain that by the end of the course you hope whatever barriers apply to them will be effectively dealt with and you will be checking with them from time to time to see how they are progressing. (The gray benchmark sheets at the back of the workbook will be useful in this regard.)

Some Assumptions About Witnessing   5 (50)

Ask the class to turn to "Three Assumptions About Witnessing" in the workbook. Go over the assumptions quickly, checking to see if the participants understand and agree with each one. Speak briefly to any questions that arise.

Ten-minute Break   10 (1:00)

The Importance of Listening   10 (1:10)

After the break, tell the class that they are now going to begin to learn to listen. "Interpersonal evangelism involves good listening and sensitive responding. So the first and most important skill in interpersonal witnessing is *listening*. What you hear determines what you say!" Ask the class to follow along in their workbooks as you read aloud "The Importance of Listening." Then go on to Exercise 7.

EXERCISE 7: Concentration 10 (1:20)

Divide the class into pairs (*A* and *B*), "Assume what you feel is a proper listening posture." Each person then comments on the other's posture. "Do you feel comfortable with each other? Now think of a time when you were annoyed about something somebody did." *A* tells *B* briefly what happened. *B* listens attentively and encouragingly. *A* then comments on *B*'s listening. Did *A* feel "heard"? Did *B*'s mannerisms facilitate communication? "Be tactful but honest!" Then reverse the roles. After each has listened and been evaluated by the other, return to the center circle.

Role Plays on Self-control 5 (1:25)

Say something like "We must learn to control the urge to speak. Good listeners are not threatened by silence, so they do not try to fill every conversational gap with words. Nor do they supply words for the person who is struggling to express his or her feelings, but instead are able to *wait* and give the other person time to get the words out. Good listeners don't feel they have to answer every question, nor do they say any more than they need to say at the moment, because they are there to listen. They are sensitive to the needs of others to be heard, and patient enough to wait for them to speak. That takes self-control."

Demonstration Role Play 1 15 (1:40)

Ask for a volunteer to do a role play with you and explain to the person privately that you want to demonstrate the right and the wrong way to listen. Ask the volunteer to make up a very sad story and to be emotional even to the point of tears in telling it, sometimes choking up. Then in front of the group you act as the listener, doing everything wrong: interrupting, breaking silences, supplying words. Invite comments from the group on what they observed.

Demonstration Role Play 2   15 (1:55)

Ask for two more volunteers, one to make up a sad tale, the other to listen properly this time (without interrupting, or breaking silences, or filling in words when the other person is struggling with strong feelings). Again invite the rest of the group to comment.

Closing   5 (2:00)

Give a quick overview of what has been covered in this session. Ask if there are any comments from the group. Close with a familiar hymn and sentence prayers. Remind them of the home assignment and dismiss them with a benediction.

WEEK FOUR

Learning to Listen

Opening Devotions *10 (10)*

Review *5 (15)*

Ask the class, "How did you do with your reading assignment? Will the exercises be helpful in improving your listening skills?" Call attention to the objectives for this week and have someone read them. Then continue "In our discussion last time we looked at two important elements of good listening: concentration and control. Picking up where we left off at our last session, we are now ready to consider another key aspect of good listening: the art of comprehension."

More Listening Skills

Comprehension *10 (25)*

Explain to the class that good listeners try to understand where the other person is coming from. Our responsibility as listeners is not to agree but to comprehend. How we relate to each other is always affected by previous experiences, theirs and ours. Listening means understanding what's going on as well as hearing what's being said. Effective interpersonal communicators are aware that there is often a large gap between one person's intentions and the other person's perceptions. It is necessary, therefore, to check our perceptions of what is going on. To do that we have to distinguish between what we see and hear and what we assume it means.

Refer to the material on perception checks in the workbook that was part of the home assignment for this week. Ask the class to suggest some of the things one might observe as one listens. List them on newsprint, as they are suggested by the group—such things as facial expressions, mannerisms, body movement, voice quality (pitch, volume, pace, intensity), posture, language, and content (information, facts, opinions, *expressed* feelings).

EXERCISE 8: Perception Check   *10 (35)*

Form groups of three. In this exercise A makes a critical judgmental statement about the church, with consistent body language. B then describes to C what he or she observed. C notes any distinctions between observed behavior and B's assumption as to its meaning. Repeat the exercise twice, rotating roles each time—that is, C makes the critical statement to A, while B observes; then B makes the critical statement to C, and A observes.

Clarification   *5 (40)*

Ask the class members to stay in their groups of three but to give you their attention, as you make some comments about clarification. "Comprehension and clarification are mutually dependent. The listener seeks clarification in order to comprehend; in comprehending, you can aid the clarification process for the other person. If you understand what's going on, you can help the other person to discover it as well, by asking sensitive questions that unlock and clarify the issues and concerns.

"The best way to clarify is to verify. Check out your observations and perceptions by repeating to the other person the substance of what you think you heard him or her say. This process, a summary of what you have heard, is called paraphrasing. Paraphrasing is not a verbatim repetition but a restatement. It communicates understanding as well as hearing. A parrot may repeat your words, but does it understand them?

"There are two objectives in paraphrasing: to check for accuracy and to communicate understanding. 'You are saying..., is that correct?' (checking your hearing of the content). 'If I understand what you're saying, you feel...' (checking your perception of the meaning)." See "Paraphrase" in the workbook for some other possible wordings. Notice the tentative way the paraphrase is presented. Tactful paraphrasing communicates to the other person a caring attitude as well as understanding.

EXERCISE 9: Paraphrasing   *15 (55)*

In the same groups each person thinks of a pet peeve, *B* relates a pet peeve to *C*, who paraphrases it back to *B*, checking for accuracy. Then *A* comments on the process, observing whether *C* has distinguished between what was heard and what was inferred and whether the paraphrasing was tactfully worded. Signal them to change roles and repeat the process twice, so that each person has taken each part.

Discussion. Regather in the big circle. Ask, "How did this last exercise go? Do you feel comfortable now with paraphrasing? Do you see the difference between paraphrasing what you hear and stating the inferences you draw from what you hear? Does this process help you to feel as if you have been listened to and understood?" The participants should answer in the affirmative. If any do not, deal with their problems or questions now.

Ten-minute Break   *10 (1:05)*

Ask the class to fill out Benchmark No. 1 during the break. (Benchmarks are at the back of each participant's book, where they may be torn out to hand in.) Collect the Benchmarks and read them after the meeting. They will give you a good picture of how the course is going and will be helpful in identifying any individual needs, questions, or concerns that should be addressed.

Review   *5 (1:10)*

Keeping the class in the big circle, summarize what has been covered in the course so far: "We've gotten acquainted; we've shared our expectations, and perhaps some are beginning to be realized; we've defined some key terms and shared our understanding of and concerns about evangelism; we've identified ways to help the church evangelize, one of which is interpersonal witnessing; we've spent considerable time on listening skills, including how to observe and how to paraphrase.

"We have also identified common barriers to our being faithful witnesses, and we have begun to deal with some of these, including those related to the meaning of evangelism, to the responsibility for evangelism, to inadequate listening skills, and to one's feeling of inadequacy."

Compassion and Commitment   15 (1:15)

So far you have been discussing human skills that can be learned. Explain to the class that there is another dimension of listening, which is not a skill but a gift of God. "It is the quality of compassion. We must listen with our hearts as well as with our ears. The word compassion literally means 'to suffer with.' It means being able to feel what the other person feels, sharing his or her agony, empathizing, suffering with the one to whom we are listening. Later in the course we shall explore what it means to be compassionate, when we role-play situations in which we encounter various human needs.

"Compassionate listening implies availability on the part of the faithful witness and a commitment to follow through in whatever way the situation calls for. The commitment is not so much a listening skill as it is a frame of mind and heart. It is the proof of one's compassion and the test of one's sincerity. Good listening must give rise to appropriate action, by which others will know they have really been heard. That is the service aspect of our evangelism, and we shall have an opportunity later in the course to see what commitment would entail in different true-to-life situations."

Qualities of a Faithful Witness

EXERCISE 10: Helpful Qualities for a Faithful Witness
10 (1:25)

A good listener is a "people" person. People persons make good witnesses, because they really care.

Ask the class to turn to Exercise 10, which lists eighteen helpful qualities for a faithful witness. No one is perfect, but the more of these qualities one has, the more effective one can be as a witness for Christ. That is not to discount the role of the Holy Spirit, who is able to work miracles despite our inadequacies. Have them take a few minutes to indicate how they would rate themselves on a scale of 0 to 10 in relation to each of the qualities, and then ask them to add the numbers to find their total numerical score. Admittedly this self-assessment is highly subjective, and it will vary every time they fill it out. Once again, what is important is not the grade they give themselves but why they grade themselves the way they do. After they have finished grading themselves, share the following:

0–25	You apparently don't see yourself as a "people person."
26–50	You may be thinking that faith-sharing is not one of your special gifts.
51–75	You may feel that faith-sharing is something you could do, but you doubt if you would enjoy it.
76–100	You realize you have better-than-average qualities for witnessing.
101–125	You are or could be a very effective witness.
126–150	You have exceptionally fine qualities for interpersonal evangelism.
151 up	You are extremely gifted as a "people" person.

It is to be hoped that most of the group, if not all, will discover they have the qualities to become effective interpersonal witnesses for Christ (if they don't think they already are) and that the remainder of the course, including the supervised calling experience, will help each person to develop her or his full potential for interpersonal evangelism.

The Indispensable Role of the Holy Spirit   5 (1:30)

Underscore for the class once again the essential role of the Holy Spirit, who is the enabler of our compassionate listening, the source of whatever effectiveness we have as witnesses, and the ultimate converter of human hearts. The style of faith-sharing this course advocates is one that recognizes our dependence on the Holy Spirit and seeks always to be open to the Spirit's leading in every evangelistic conversation. All discussion of our human qualities and techniques must be viewed and understood in that light.

The Use of Questions in Witnessing   5 (1:35)

Say to the class something like this: "One of our assumptions about interpersonal evangelism was that it involves sensitive sharing as well as good listening. Sensitive sharing calls for another interpersonal communication skill: the ability to ask questions appropriately and tactfully. That means not appearing to pry or sounding like an interrogator. You have read about and have had an opportunity to practice this skill in your home assignment for this week.

"Asking the right questions at the right time and in the right way encourages response and facilitates communication. It is indispensable to effective faith-sharing, because, if carefully done, it can deepen the level of conversation and lead to reflection and insights that are helpful to self-understanding and decision-making."

The Paradoxical Nature of Faith   5 (1:40)

"A little later we shall do some more exercises on the art of asking questions, but first we need to talk about faith, since an understanding of faith is crucial to a faith-sharing approach to interpersonal evangelism. Religious faith, simply defined, is believing in the existence of and trusting in the goodness of a Supreme Being, however understood. Christians believe that God was revealed sufficiently for the salvation of the world in the person of Jesus Christ. Christian faith means trusting in Jesus as one's Savior and following him as one's Lord.

"The paradox of faith is that while the Bible on the one hand lays upon us the responsibility of believing in Christ, on the other hand it affirms very definitely that faith is a gift of God. This tension between the givenness of faith and our responsibility to believe ('the gift and the grasp' of faith) is clearly seen when one examines the way faith and belief are treated in the New Testament."

EXERCISE 11: The Paradox of Faith 15 (1:55)

Ask the class to turn to Exercise 11 and, in the blank space before each text, put a small "g" if the text seems to emphasize the "grasp" side of the paradox (our responsibility to have faith), and a large "G" if it supports the givenness of faith.

Discussion. When the class members have finished the exercise, let them share their answers. In general, the texts which emphasize our human responsibility (small "g" for "grasp") are nos. 1, 2, 4, 5, 9, 10, 11, 12, 16, 17, 20, 22, and 24. Those which seem to stress the givenness of faith (large "G" for "gift") are nos. 3, 6, 7, 8, 13, 14, 15, 18, 19, 21, and 23. Some of the texts may reflect both sides of the paradox. Ask if they can see the tension between these two dimensions of faith. It is, nevertheless, a "pseudo-paradox," for if there is a God, then ultimately faith has to be a gift, for it is our response to the God who reaches out to us. We struggle to believe, and while we are struggling, we think it all depends on us. In a sense it does, for we have the freedom to say yes or no to God. But once we believe, we know that our faith is indeed a response and that God was there long before we ever believed in God. But we know that only *after* the fact, with the hindsight of faith.

Closing 5 (2:00)

Call attention to the home assignment for next week and encourage the class members to pray for one another as they continue together in the course. Then join hands for a closing hymn, a few sentence prayers, and the Lord's Prayer, followed by a benediction.

WEEK FIVE

Probing
Our Faith

Opening Devotions   *10 (10)*

Choose one of the suggested devotionals in the workbook or plan your own. You might sing a hymn or two, have someone read an appropriate scripture passage, invite people to share what they would like to praise God for today, and close by singing the Doxology.

Review   *5 (15)*

Say to the class, "We have been discussing the meaning of faith, and we have seen that there is a tension between our responsibility to have faith and our dependence upon God for the gift of faith." Ask if they have thought further about that. Are there any questions? "Continuing the exploration of faith, look at the goals for this session. Note the reference to the concept of a 'leap of faith.' Though we say faith is a gift, we sense that we have to take the 'leap.'"

The Leap of Faith   *10 (25)*

The diagram with that title in the workbook is a helpful teaching tool for describing graphically the concept of the leap of faith in relation to the gift-grasp paradox. Familiarize yourself with the explanation so you can lead the class through it now.

After covering the main points, give the participants a chance to ask any questions they may have. Point out "The Gift, the Grasp, and the Leap of Faith" in the workbook and suggest that they reread it carefully at home so that they can explain it to someone else.

The *What* and the *Why* of Faith   10 (35)

To be a faithful and effective witness you must know what you believe and why you believe it. People do not generally recognize or understand the difference between the *what* and the *why* of faith. When asked why they believe in God, their answers are usually "what" answers. It is in fact impossible to say why you believe in God without using faith statements, which are in effect circular arguments that presuppose what they are claiming to prove. In logical discourse such statements are called "tautologies." A tautological statement is repetitious, one that is necessarily true by virtue of its structure.

Faith statements are also subjective—that is, they are not self-evident to a nonbeliever. So instead of trying to prove God by adding up the facts and arriving at a conclusion (deductive reasoning), you answer the *why* question by admitting you can't prove God and that your faith is the starting point, not the conclusion (confessing your faith assumptions), and then, after winning the right to be heard, you can share what is *for you* the confirming evidence of your faith assumption (i.e., your personal experience of God). What you say is intended not as a convincing proof to the questioner but as the justification or reinforcement of your own conviction.

What statements are affirmational and have to do with your beliefs about God. *Why* statements should be confessional in tone, having to do with your personal experiences of God. The objective of telling *what* you believe is to be understood. The objective of saying *why* you believe is to be believable. The *what* gives clarity to the *why*; the *why* gives integrity to the *what*.

Why statements are also, ultimately, *what* statements, because they too are faith statements! But they are more clearly so and more obviously circular (redundant, tautological), whereas *what* statements are more dogmatic, and those who utter them in response to the question *why?* are seemingly unaware of their tautological nature. One clue to identifying *why* statements is their experiential quality; they tend to be statements about oneself, whereas *what* statements tend to be about the content of one's belief. Sometimes the "whatness" is veiled; that is, some *what* statements have to be dissected in order for their "whatness" to be detected.

After explaining the *what* and the *why* of faith to the participants, ask if they have any questions, before beginning the next exercise.

EXERCISE 12: Answering the *What* and the *Why* Questions   *10 (45)*

In the blank space before each statement, participants are to indicate which kind of statement they think it is by writing "what" (beliefs about God) or "why" (confirming evidence of a faith assumption). After they have finished, ask how they responded to each statement. ("How many said 'what'? How many said 'why'?") Deal with any questions that arise before moving on to the next statement. They will discover that putting a "because" before a *what* statement does not make it a *why* statement!

Some of the statements are quite obviously one or the other. Statements 1, 4, 6, 7, 9, 10, 12, 14, and 15 are clearly *what* statements. Nos. 2, 3, 5, 8, 11, 17, and 20 are clearly *why* statements. No. 13, when disssected, is seen to be a *what* statement: "I believe in Jesus and I believe that what he taught is true." No. 16 is also a *what* statement: It says, in effect, "God is the First Cause." It is a statement of what one believes about God, not why one believes in God. Similarly, No. 18 belongs with the *what* statements: "I believe the answer to the ultimate *why* is God." (It evokes another question: But why do you believe that?) No. 19 is tricky. It is a frequently heard statement that is partly *what* ("I believe in Jesus") and would appear to be partly *why* ("because I grew up in a Christian home"). The *why* part, however, leaves the other person with an unanswered question: "But why do you believe in Jesus *now?*"

When you have quickly run through the statements, take a break.

Five-minute Break   5 *(50)*

Review   5 *(55)*

It will be helpful here to review what you have covered so far in this session. For example: "We have been exploring the meaning of faith. We have tried to understand the paradox between our freedom to believe or not to believe and our dependence upon God, who is the source of our faith, the tension between our grasp and God's gift. It is ultimately, however, a pseudo-paradox, since the gift always precedes the grasp. If we take seriously the givenness of faith, the implications are tremendous for the way we witness, preach, teach, evangelize— indeed, for however we share our faith. We confess that faith is not something we can make ourselves 'have'; faith is something we find ourselves with. If we can't make ourselves 'have' it, how can we make anyone else 'have' it? The expression 'confession of faith' takes on a new meaning!"

Continuing your comments to the class: "We also said it is important to know the difference between the *what* and the *why* of faith, and we analyzed some statements to see under which of those two categories we would classify them. The distinction is important in interpersonal witnessing, for we should not answer the *why* question as if it were a *what* question. Too many would-be evangelists make that mistake.

"In order to get a feel for the distinction between the *what* and the *why*, we're now going to do some exercises. First let's look at the relationship between faith and doubt."

Faith and Doubt

EXERCISE 13: The Faith–Doubt Continuum   20 *(1:15)*

Divide the participants into threes for the next three exercises. Ask them to turn to the Faith–Doubt Continuum in the workbook and mark the line according to the instructions. When they have finished, they are to tell the others in their triad why they put the marks where they did. Remind them to practice good listening skills as they share with each other.

Once again, their explanations are more important than the placement of the dates.

Discussion. When they have finished explaining their diagrams to one another, point out that they have just *stated* their faith (*that* they believe, to whatever extent). They have also seen that faith and doubt go together, and that their faith has its ups and downs. Ask, simply as a matter of interest, how many of them brought Jesus Christ into their answer. Are there any general observations to be made as a result of this exercise? Consider such questions as these:

> To what circumstances are our high and low points related?
> When do we tend to feel closest to God?
> When do we tend to feel farthest from God?
> What is the relationship between faith and doubt?
> What is the relationship between faith as reliance upon God and faith as belief in God?

Practice in Faith-sharing

EXERCISE 14: Answering the *What* Question   10 (1:25)

You might introduce this section as follows: "We have not yet discussed the content of our faith—that is, *what* we believe. Most people have certain religious beliefs, some more clearly defined and developed than others. This exercise gives you an opportunity to state these beliefs as succinctly and clearly as you can.

"Tell the others in your triad *what* you as a Christian believe— that is, the content of your faith, your basic beliefs. Each person will have three minutes. When you hear my signal it will be the next person's turn to do the same thing."

EXERCISE 15: Answering the *Why* Question   20 (1:45)

Without any preliminary discussion, begin this exercise as follows: "Identify yourselves as *A*, *B*, or *C*. In this exercise *B* is a believer, *A* is an agnostic, and *C* is an observer. *A* asks *B*, 'Why do you believe in Jesus Christ?' *B* responds and *C* observes without comment. When you hear my signal, C should comment on what she or he has observed."

Now ask them to switch roles and repeat the process twice, so that each person has had an opportunity to be in each role. Give them a signal to indicate when the observers should comment, and when they should switch roles for the third go-round.

Discussion. After the observers have spoken, you ask, "How did it go? Any comments from the observers? Could you tell the difference between the *what* and the *why*? Was B using 'why' statements? Was B 'confessional' (confessing his or her faith assumption and then sharing personal experiences as 'confirming evidence')? Was B convincing? Appealing? Preachy? Dogmatic? How did you agnostics feel?" Don't spend too much time on this. Just get a few general comments.

Review   10 (1:55)

Regather in the main circle and ask for comments on this session's exercises. In addition to discussion on the nature of their faith statements, you also want to find out whether they have been using their listening skills. Ask who did most of the talking, the believers or the agnostics? (Instead of answering A's question immediately, it would have been appropriate in this situation for B first to have become a listener by asking tactfully why A wanted to know; B needs to know where A is coming from before answering. Remind them that the instruction was for B to "respond," not monopolize the conversation. It would be proper for B in this case to respond with a question, rather than with an answer.

Closing   5 (2:00)

Join hands and with heads bowed invite the members of the class to say whatever words express how they are feeling at that moment. Then offer a brief closing prayer and give the benediction. Remind them of the assignment for next week.

WEEK SIX

Sharing
Our Faith

Opening Devotions 5 (5)

There is a very full agenda for this session, so plan a shorter devotional today.

Review 5 (10)

Ask if there are questions about what was covered last week. Then call attention to the objectives and alert the class that there is more to cover this time than usual.

Faith-sharing Defined and Described 5 (15)

Last week all participants had an opportunity to share their faith with two other persons. The style of interpersonal evangelism this course advocates involves a faith-sharing approach; faith-sharing was defined in the first meeting as "three-way communication in which two or more people relate to each other their personal experiences of God." (Write this on a sheet of newsprint and put it up on the wall for everyone to see.) In the process both persons reexperience the reality of God (hence, "*three*-way communication"). Faith-sharing is nonthreatening. It does not put the other person on the defensive. It is not judgmental or dogmatic. The witness is freed from the burden of having to argue someone into the kingdom or of trying to prove the existence of God. Instead, the witness must first be a listener and then "plug into" the other person's experience.

Faith speaks to faith. It's a heart-to-heart, not head-to-head, conversation. The witness must know how and when to share his or her own faith story. It should never be imposed upon the other person, but shared only when the witness has won the right to be heard.

Some Premises for Faith-sharing   *10 (25)*

While everyone is still in the large circle, ask them to turn to "Premises for Faith-sharing," the basic assumptions upon which the faith-sharing approach to interpersonal evangelism is based. Read them aloud. Ask if there are any questions. Call attention to the passages they read in the workbook as part of their assignment for this week. What insights about faith-sharing did they gain from the biblical texts?

EXERCISE 16: Sharing Faith Stories   *20 (45)*

Now divide the participants into new groups of four and ask them to think for a moment about their most recent experience of God. Put it this way: "Think of a moment when you felt very close to God—the most recent time when God was very real to you. Why did you feel that way? What was happening at the time? Tell the other members of your group, who should be active listeners. Each person has four minutes to tell his or her faith story. I'll let you know when it's time for the next person to speak."

Discussion. Regroup in the center circle. Ask, "How did it go with your faith-sharing? What did you learn from this experience? Did the others listen well to you? How did you feel about one another's faith stories?" Invariably it is a positive experience. Ask if they were made to feel defensive or threatened, "judged" by what they heard. Comment that people are seldom if ever offended when you share your faith sensitively and sincerely. "Being sensitive means not imposing it on the other person but rather waiting for the proper moment, having earned the right to be heard. Faith-sharing, remember, is three-way communication. The Christian witness hopes the other person will share his or her faith at whatever level and to whatever extent that person is moved to do and, when the person does so, responds appropriately. An appropriate response could be anything from a nod or a smile to the sharing of one's own faith story; from a direct answer to another question. Such an approach is consistent with a style of evangelism that is *service* oriented, where the task of the witness is not to unload but to listen and where words are backed by deeds."

Five-minute Break   *5 (50)*

Five Points for Faith-sharing   *5 (55)*

"Part of your home assignment for this week was to read the article entitled 'Five Points for Faith-sharing.' Please turn to the end of the article, where the points are summarized. We're going to review them now and do some exercises that will help us see how they work.

"With regard to faith-sharing, one question we need to address is, 'When is it proper to share one's faith? How does one begin?' A more appropriate way to put the question for someone who understands the importance of listening would be, 'How does one get the *other* person to share?' Or, to put it yet another way, 'How does one turn an ordinary conversation into a faith-sharing experience?' The answer is by the sensitive use of questions, a listening skill to which we have already referred, but which we have not yet discussed or practiced in class, although you did the workbook exercise on Creative Questions as one of your home assignments.

"The word 'point' has a double meaning, referring both to a conversational moment calling for a particular response on the part of the witness and to the idea, statement, or action on the part of the other person which precipitates that moment."

EXERCISE 17: Come-in Points   *15 (1:10)*

There are more opportunities than aspiring witnesses sometimes realize to ask a question that can instantly transform an ordinary conversation into a faith-sharing experience. These are the come-in points for which every sensitive witness should be listening. If, for example, the other person has shared some tragic news, the witness might ask, "What has that done to your faith?" The question may evoke a beautiful affirmation of faith or an outburst of anger against God. Either way, it is a faith response to a faith question. Such a question, sensitively and caringly asked, does not threaten others or put them on the defensive. Rather, it allows them to respond at whatever level of faith they may be at the moment.

Divide the participants into groups of four and assign each of the groups an equal number of the twenty statements listed in Exercise 17. Get them to indicate how they would respond to these typical come-in points, which one might hear in an ordinary conversation, by writing a faith question in the space provided for each point assigned them.

Discussion. After they have completed the exercise, let some of them share their answers. The less structured the questions, the better. Low-structured questions give the other person plenty of room to respond, whereas high-structured questions, like those demanding a yes or no answer, are limiting. Faith questions are "invitational"; you invite, then listen. The beauty of this approach is its simplicity. It is amazing how easy it is to be on a faith-sharing level with someone, even strangers. The witness listens actively until there is an appropriate moment for a personal faith response. These are the plug-in points, calling for a second type of response.

Plug-in Points   15 (1:25)

"Plug-in points are the switchboard of the faith-sharing exchange, the sockets where your faith can plug into the other person's faith experience. In interpersonal witnessing this is the point you are always hoping to attain. The task here is relational. You affirm and relate to the other person's faith experience, being careful not to overpower or overshadow the person. The goal is to encourage that person to share his or her faith [come in]. There will be an opportunity for you to tell your story [plug in], but first you must be a listener."

Role Play 1 (To demonstrate how to ask a faith question and

how to plug into another person's negative faith experience).
Ask for a volunteer, A, to do a role-play demonstration with
you. Privately you tell A to play the role of someone who is
emotionally upset. You will ask, "Are you OK?" A nods. You
ask, "Do you want to talk about it?" A pours out a hard-luck
story. You ask a faith question. A responds with a strong denun-
ciation of God: "Where is God? Why would God let this happen
to me? How can people say God is good when God lets things
like this happen?" That's your plug-in point, but don't answer
until you're sure A has unloaded whatever it is he or she is
thinking. Then you say something like, "I've never gone through
anything like that, but I can understand why you're angry at
God." Affirm; relate. A doesn't want your explanation. What A
wants is your understanding. Wait for a response and then play
it by ear. Explain the situation to the class as follows: "We're
sitting at the same table in the company cafeteria. We know
each other, but not well." You need not spend more than four or
five minutes on this enactment.

Role Play 2 (To demonstrate another come-in point and how
to plug into a positive faith experience). After giving the class a
chance to comment, ask for two more volunteers to do another
demonstration. Privately tell A and B that they are neighbors. B
belongs to Central Presbyterian Church; A is unchurched. B
calls on A after learning of the death of A's spouse. B listens as A
grieves, then asks a faith question. A responds with a positive
affirmation of faith and wonders if B can understand that, know-
ing that A never goes to church. That's the plug-in point for B to
affirm and relate to A's faith. Set the stage for the class as follows:
"A and B are neighbors. B is calling on A at home. We pick up
the conversation just after they have sat down in the living
room."

Discussion. After four or five minutes, give the demonstrators a chance to comment on the experience and then ask for
comments from the class. How did they think it went? Did B
respond appropriately? If not, what should B's response have
been? B should by all means affirm A for drawing close to God in
this time of sorrow. Point out to the class that it would also be
appropriate for B to offer to pray at the conclusion of such a

faith-sharing visit. After thanking the demonstrators, return to a discussion of the remaining three points.

Take-on Points   *10 (1:40)*

Take-on points are confrontational, their purpose being to challenge a faith contradiction. There are times when it is appropriate to help the other person see the unreasonableness or the logical inconsistency of something he or she has said, by asking a question which points up that inconsistency. For example, to the person who claims to believe in Christ but never goes to church, you might say, "How does not going to church relate to your belief in Christ?" (low-structured question); or, "Is not going to church a good way to show you believe in Christ?" (high-structured question).

Two rules to remember here are: (1) that you can say the hard thing if your face and body language communicate a loving attitude and a caring spirit, and if you have listened carefully and responded caringly to other hurts and feelings that may have fueled the inconsistency; and (2) that you can and should be up front with your feelings ("I'm ashamed that after living next door to you all these years I've just now gotten around to inviting you to church"). Take-on points are confrontational, but not in the sense of evoking antagonism or conflict. On the contrary, you appeal to reason rather than resort to attack or counterattack. Criticism is not necessarily a take-on point. The best way to respond to attack is to look for whatever points of agreement you can find in the other person's statement. It's a way of cushioning the blow and defusing anger. You can often turn a criticism into a compliment by responding in a nondefensive, reasonable manner. It is also important not to react to critical generalities; always try for specifics by asking questions that help the other person focus his or her complaint. (Review the article "Responding to Criticism," pp. 31–33.)

As leader, you can illustrate a take-on point as follows: "A resident complains to a visitor from the church that no one ever calls. The visitor, appealing to reason in a friendly, nonthreatening manner, says, 'But *we're* here . . . ?'" (Face language is important in such a response!) Or the visitor could ask a low-structured question, such as "How do you feel about *our* being here?"

Take-off Points   *10 (1:50)*

There are also conversational take-off points. These are times when we need to clarify, explain, or inform. That does not mean, however, saying everything all at once. We don't have to tell the whole story in response to the first question we're asked. Rather, we try to say whatever is helpful and necessary and then wait for a response. "The object is not to belabor the take-off point but to find another plug-in point. The witness should not be trapped into becoming a question answerer."

The simplest way to illustrate how to move from a take-off point to a come-in point is to suggest that, after answering a number of questions, the witness might say something like this: "I know I can't answer all your questions. But even if I could, how would that affect your faith?" The question can be worded any number of ways, the object being to bring the conversation back to the faith-sharing level.

"There is another rule for this style of interpersonal witnessing: It is better to ask questions than to give answers. Answers deny the other person the joy of discovery. Contradictory statements tend to force the other person into a defensive position; they evoke the need to defend a point of view. Sensitive questioning, on the other hand, can help people to verbalize those assumptions and to discover whether or not their conclusions are consistent with their assumptions. You will know that you have been asking the right questions when someone says, 'I see what you mean,' and you have never said what you mean! The other person has simply recognized the logical conclusion implied in the answer to the question you asked. What is recommended, therefore, is a Socratic approach to witnessing: asking questions that help the other person to discover the answers for himself or herself.

"As should be apparent from what has been said about them, the first four points of faith-sharing are by no means mutually exclusive. In the dynamics of interpersonal witnessing, the conversation can bounce from point to point. There is a time to affirm and a time to inform, a time to invite and a time to relate, a time to explain and a time to confront, a time to speak and a time to listen."

Decide-to Points   *10 (2:00)*

To introduce this concept you could say something along these lines: "A decide-to point is that moment in a faith-sharing conversation when it is appropriate for you, the witness, to invite a faith decision, again by asking a high-structured but sensitively worded question. It is an appeal for the other person to make a choice in the context of faith, a choice informed by one's desire to put one's trust in God. It is asking a person to commit herself or himself, believing that in so doing she or he is opting for God. A faith decision is a choice in which one's belief in God is put to the test. It is taking the next step toward God or deciding in obedience to God. Once that is done, your proper response is to confirm the other person in his or her faith decision and to assure the person of your support in that choice. Decide-to points are invitational, not coercive."

Ask the class to turn to "Inviting a Faith Decision." Go through the guidelines, inviting comments or questions. Tell them they will have an opportunity to practice these rules when they are role-playing, especially during the last two weeks of the course. There will also be ample opportunity to apply this skill, along with all the others we've been learning, during the supervised calling experience. Asking for a faith decision is an extremely important aspect of interpersonal evangelism, for without an invitation to respond in some appropriate way, one's witness is incomplete. Note the style that is recommended for inviting people to make a faith decision. It calls for sensitivity as well as forthrightness on the part of the witness, not to miss the moment.

EXERCISE 18: A Faith-sharing Conversation   *10 (2:10)*

Divide the participants into groups of three. *A* and *B* are neighbors. *A* is ecstatic at having just won a million dollars in the state lottery. *B* doesn't know that. They meet on their front sidewalk Saturday morning. *B* is a Presbyterian; *A* is unchurched. They have never had a faith-sharing conversation. *B* greets *A* cheerily. "What's new?" In the conversation that follows, *B* should use good listening skills and be as sensitive as possible to the five points for faith-sharing. *A* has to leave after four or five minutes. *C* is the hidden observer who at the end of the conversation will comment on the exchange, noting *B*'s use of questions and other interpersonal witnessing skills. Were there any come-in points? Plug-in points? Take-on points? Take-off points? Did *B* respond appropriately? Was *B* able to turn the conversation into a faith-sharing experience? What, if anything, could *B* have done differently? How did the conversation end? Was there a decide-to point? What is the next step for *B* to take?

Closing 5 (2:15)

Regather in the center circle for a brief closing prayer. Call attention to the home assignment for next week. Ask the class to take a few moments to fill out Benchmark No. 2 and remove it from their workbooks before they leave. Collect them for your later perusal.

WEEK SEVEN

Understanding the Gospel

Opening Devotions *10 (10)*

Review *10 (20)*

You may want to begin with a few comments about the completed Benchmarks. Do they indicate progress? Needs? Problems? Under the personal barriers to witnessing identified in Exercise 6 was a group relating to faith problems. Ask, "Has our probe of the nature and role of faith for the past two or three weeks been helpful in overcoming those barriers?" After a brief discussion call attention to the objectives for this session.

Your review may then proceed along the following lines: "Summarizing briefly what was covered last week, we have been trying to understand and practice a faith-sharing approach to interpersonal evangelism. Last time we paid particular attention to the use of questions, in relation to the five points for faith-sharing: come-in points, plug-in points, take-on points, take-off points, and decide-to points. The interpersonal communication skills we are learning can be used whenever and wherever we are in conversation with another person. They represent not a method but a style, not a technique but a way of relating to other human beings.

"Early in the course we said that although not everyone is gifted as an evangelist, everyone is a witness and there is something everyone can do to help the church evangelize. To that end we have been trying to develop our interpersonal communication skills and to learn how to share our faith. In order to be effective witnesses we need to understand the *what* of *the* Faith as well as the *why* of our faith. So far we have been concentrating more on the *why* than on the *what*, which is consistent with an evangelistic approach that is more relational than informational, more incarnational than propositional. We reach out to others in the name of a Savior and Lord who came not to be served but to serve.

"But how will people know that, unless somebody tells them? We have good news to share, but from whom will they hear it? It is important to be a good listener and encourage others to share their faith. It is also essential to know how to share the good news of Jesus Christ. That is precisely what evangelism is: sharing the good news! In this session we shall concentrate on the message itself."

Definition and Content of the Gospel

"What is the good news? Part of the home assignment for this week was to read the article on that subject in the workbook. As we continue to wrestle with that question, let's keep in mind the people to whom we bear witness, so that we are always thinking about how what we say is good news for the person to whom we're speaking.

"As the article pointed out, the word 'evangel' is the Greek *euaggelion* [write it on the board], translated 'gospel,' or 'good news.' The word 'gospel' is a contraction of two Anglo-Saxon terms *god*, meaning 'God' or 'good,' and *spell*, meaning 'tale' or 'tidings': 'good news.' So evangelism is doing the evangel, promulgating good news in word and deed. Our good news, our gospel, is the good news of Jesus Christ.

"The personal qualities we discussed earlier are important assets for faith sharers, but if we are going to be effective witnesses for Jesus Christ, we really have to understand what the gospel is and know how to communicate it faithfully." John R. W. Stott has provided a helpful way of understanding the gospel by identifying several of its elements, which have been expanded somewhat and incorporated under the heading "Aspects of the Gospel." The class will now have an opportunity to discuss in depth the various aspects of the gospel.

Aspects of the Gospel

EXERCISE 19: The Gospel Events   *20 (40)*

The first thing we need to know is the gospel story, the facts of Jesus' life. Jesus' life has its own self-authenticating evangelistic impact. The Holy Spirit works in and through the story to touch the hearts of its hearers. The Living Word comes to us through the inspired written words that relate the story of a crucified and risen Savior.

Divide the participants into groups of four, with one person to serve as the recorder in each group. Ask them to list on sheets of newsprint everything they know about the events of Jesus' life, who he was, where he came from, what he did, what happened to him. Allow about ten minutes for this task.

Discussion. When the time is up, ask them to put their sheets up on the wall. The lists should be fairly similar, covering the basic events of Jesus' life. Note the difference between the factual statements about events and any affirmations of faith that are listed, such as "He is the way, and the truth, and the life," or "He is the Savior of the world." This is the God-spell, the good story, and they should be able to tell it.

But to whom? Ask the class, "Who would be most likely to respond to the gospel story?" They would be on target if they say children, who love to hear the story of Jesus; and godly people of other faiths, who are always impressed by the person and life of Jesus. This is an important plug-in point for interfaith dialogue. Believers also respond to the Jesus story, as Katherine Hankey's gospel song (*HL* 443) reminds us:

I love to tell the story;
  For those who know it best
Seem hungering and thirsting
  To hear it, like the rest.

EXERCISE 20: Witnesses to the Gospel   *25 (1:05)*

The next question is, How do you know that the story is true? Ask the class, "What if after hearing the Jesus story, someone asked you, 'What evidence is there?' What would you say?"

The Scriptures. Someone in the class will usually come up
with the first and most obvious answer: the Bible. Ask them,
"Where in the Bible is the Jesus story told?" Do they have any
problems with the discrepancies among the different accounts?
Point out that the Gospels are not to be viewed as historical
biographies but as faith portraits. Each writer was painting a
picture of Jesus as he saw him, emphasizing what for him were
the important features. Though they differ in some minor details,
there is a remarkable harmony and consistency among them, so
that the composite picture of our Lord is beautifully integrated
and powerfully convincing.

The fact is that for centuries the Bible has been subjected to
more intensive critical analysis and scientific scrutiny than any
other book written, all of which has not diminished but rather
increased its value as "the unique and authoritative witness to
Jesus Christ," according to our Presbyterian ordination vows. It
is God's word to us today, as it has been to Christians in ages
past. The written word bears witness to the Living Word who
"became flesh and dwelt among us, full of grace and truth" (John
1:14).

Divide the scripture passages in Exercise 20, Part One,
equally among the small groups and ask participants to write
down what insights they might gain from the passages assigned
them.

Discussion. Regather in the center circle and ask the recorders to share *briefly* what their groups learned from their respective passages regarding the witness of the scriptures.

The Eyewitnesses. Point out that in addition to the written
record itself, there were the recorded testimonies of eyewitnesses.
Perhaps someone already will have mentioned them. Ask different persons to read each of the following passages aloud, to give
the class a feel for the importance the Bible attaches to these
eyewitness accounts: John 1:14; Acts 10:39, 41; Acts 26:15–16; 1
Cor. 15:15–8; 1 John 1:1–4. You may want to comment briefly
after each reading. Have the class write "The Eyewitnesses" in
the space provided in Exercise 20, Part Two.

When they have finished, say, "As you think about sharing
the good news, what kind of people might be particularly

impressed by this kind of evidence?" Appropriate answers would be: people who already believe and want confirming evidence; people who are struggling with doubt and whose faith needs reinforcing; reasoning people, who want to be convinced. "Any others?"

The Holy Spirit. "In addition to the scriptures and the eyewitnesses, there is yet another witness, the one who authenticates all others and without whose testimony no one could believe. Who would that be?" Someone will probably come up with the answer right away: the Holy Spirit. This should be written after Part Three in Exercise 20. Ask different persons to read the following passages to underscore the Spirit's role as witness: Rom. 8:16; Heb. 10:15; 1 John 5:7.

Ten-minute Break   *10 (1:15)*

The Gospel Affirmations   *5 (1:20)*

"What is it the witnesses want the world to know about Jesus? What do they say about him?" Probably the class will immediately come up with the two basic affirmations of the gospel, that Jesus is Lord and Jesus is Savior. You might prompt them by asking, "What is every person asked when she or he joins the church? What are parents asked when their baby is baptized?" ("Do you accept Jesus Christ as your personal Lord and Savior?" or words to that effect.) Have someone read aloud Romans 10:9, and someone else 1 John 4:14. These are the two basic affirmations of faith that define our relationship to Jesus Christ. He is the Savior of the world and our personal Savior; he is Lord of the universe and Lord of our lives.

Ask, "Who in particular needs to hear this aspect of the gospel?" Certainly the answer would include those who are wrestling with the decision to join the church; they need to take seriously what it means to accept him as their Savior and to follow him as their Lord. Churches need to give integrity to the process of receiving new members, who should be able to take their vows with integrity, having thought through the implications. In the once widely used *Book of Common Worship*, those who join the church on confession of faith are asked, "Do you promise with the aid of the Holy Spirit to be Christ's faithful disciples to your life's end? . . . and to give your whole heart to the service of Christ and his kingdom throughout the world?" (p. 132). Ask, "What does it mean to be Christ's woman or man in the world today?"

EXERCISE 21: The Promises of the Gospel   *30 (1:50)*

The Promise of Forgiveness. Next there are the gospel promises. Ask, "Why is the affirmation that Jesus is Savior and Lord good news?" After they mention a few things, you might say (if no one else does) that one reason the affirmations are good news is that if Jesus *is* Savior and Lord, he can produce on his promises! The gospel has answers for the three basic problems of humanity. First there's the problem of sin. If there is a God, then how can we prove ourselves acceptable to God? We know we can't, for as Paul declared, quoting the psalmist, "None is righteous, no, not one" (Rom. 3:10) and "all have sinned and fall short of the glory of God" (Rom. 3:23). Ask, "What is the gospel's answer to the problem of sin?" The answer, of course, is the promise of forgiveness.

The Promise of Eternal Life. The second basic human problem is our mortality. Life is a one-way street, at the end of which the Grim Reaper awaits us all. If all our striving for fame and fortune must one day be frustrated by the finality of death, all is indeed vanity, as the writer of Ecclesiastes concluded. What is the gospel's answer to the problem of death? The class will know that it is the promise of eternal life.

The Promise to Be with Us. Jesus did not come to tell us how to die, however, but to show us how to live. "I came," he said, "that they may have life, and have it abundantly" (John 10:10). The third basic problem of humanity is how to cope with all the pressures and problems of our daily lives. What is the gospel's answer to the problem of coping?" It is Jesus' promise to be with us always, fulfilled in the gift of the Holy Spirit.

Divide the participants into three groups. Ask them to write, in the spaces provided in Exercise 21, the three basic promises of the gospel. Under each promise there is a list of scripture passages; each group is to focus on the list of passages under just one of the headings, assigned to you. The members of the group are to look up the passages and see what light they shed on that particular gospel promise. One person functions as the recorder for each group. After they look up each scripture reference, they are to identify the kinds of people who might be especially responsive to that aspect of the gospel.

Discussion. Ask the recorders to summarize the results of their Bible study. Give the other members of each group a chance to add more if they wish, then move on to the next group. After the three groups have reported, ask the class if they have a deeper appreciation of the promises of the gospel. "Do you understand why it is good news?"

Closing   *10 (2:00)*

Summarize what has been covered in this session. Ask if there are any final comments or questions from the class. As part of the closing exercises, invite the class to share what aspect of the gospel is particularly meaningful to them at this point in their lives and, if they're willing, to say why it is so meaningful. This could be a most inspirational time, at the end of which all could stand, join hands, and close with sentence prayers related to what each has shared. While still standing with heads bowed, sing (*HB* 535):

Hear our prayer, O Lord, Hear our prayer, O Lord,
Incline thine ear to us, And grant us thy peace.

You could conclude with the words "through Jesus Christ our Lord. Amen."

WEEK EIGHT

Exploring the Kingdom

Opening Devotions   *10 (10)*

Review   *5 (15)*

Last week we considered several different aspects of the gospel, each of which might have particular relevance for different people and for different reasons: the gospel events, the gospel witnesses, the gospel affirmations, and the gospel promises. It is important to keep these different elements in mind when we're engaged in interpersonal evangelism, so that our presentation of the gospel will be relevant to the other person's needs. Ask, "Would anyone like to share any thoughts he or she may have had since the last session?" If there are no comments, have someone read today's objectives.

More Aspects of the Gospel

EXERCISE 22: The Gospel Conditions   *25 (40)*

We ended last week with the gospel promises. Today we begin with this question: Are the promises of the gospel automatic, or are there things we must do to receive them? We talk about God's unconditional grace, love with no strings attached. Yet Jesus seems to impose certain conditions for receiving the promises. Are there strings or no strings? Was the young man's question to Jesus—"Teacher, what must I do to inherit eternal life?" (Mark 10:17)—a legitimate one? Was the Philippian jailer off the mark when he asked Paul and Silas, "What must I do to be saved?" (Acts 16:30)? What about the conditions of the gospel? What must *we* do to receive the promises?

Form the class into three groups. Ask them to turn in the workbook to Exercise 22. Divide the list of scripture references equally among the groups and ask them to see how they would answer the aforementioned questions in the light of the scripture passages they have just read. Follow the instructions for the exercise.

Discussion. Regather in the center circle. Ask the recorders to report for each group. Use a sheet of newsprint to list the things they mention, which will include such words as repentance, faith, baptism, patient endurance, worthy deeds, keeping the commandments, and public profession of faith.

The Meaning of Repentance   10 (50)

"The New Testament Greek word for repentance is *metanoia* [write it on the board], which conveys the idea of a change of mind and heart. *Metonoia* expresses the rich meaning of the prophetic concept of conversion, the Hebrew word for which was *shub*. It occurs more than a thousand times in the Old Testament and almost always conveys the idea of 'returning' or 'going back again.' Since the prophets viewed sin as turning away from God, so conversion (*shub*) was understood as turning *back* to God. It involved obedience to God's will, unconditional trust in God, and the renunciation of everything ungodly. Repentance is not just saying you're sorry, or feeling sorry, but determining to do something about it! It is essential to being converted, the Greek word for which is *epistrepho* [write it for them to see], which implies a complete turnaround, a new orientation, a new focus, a totally new commitment.

"To whom might the conditions of the gospel be especially relevant? The answer would certainly include those who are looking for 'cheap grace.' We were bought for a costly price, as the apostle Paul reminds us (1 Cor. 6:20; 7:23), by one who 'humbled himself and became obedient unto death, even death on a cross' (Phil. 2:8) and who bids us to deny ourselves and take up our cross and follow him (Matt. 16:24; Mark 8:34; Luke

9:23). The gospel conditions are the answer to those who are wondering 'What must I do to be saved?' We know, of course, that God is able to save whomever he will, despite our faults and failures. God's love can transcend all conditions."

The Gospel Demands   5 *(55)*

Explain to the class that the demands of the gospel include, of course, everything Jesus requires of his followers. It is living one's life in obedience to Christ. It is taking seriously what it means to accept Jesus Christ as the Lord of one's life. These requirements embrace all of Jesus' teachings, but they can be summed up in two overarching demands, the Great Commandment and the Great Commission.

The Great Commandment. The conditions for receiving the gospel promises become the gospel demands upon those who accept it. "If you love me," said Jesus, "you will keep my commandments. . . . This is my commandment, that you love one another" (John 14:15; 15:12). In his response to the man who asked him what was the greatest commandment, Jesus indicated the nature and extent of the love he demands of his followers: You shall love the Lord your God with all your heart, soul, mind, and strength, and your neighbor as yourself (Mark 12:30–31).

The Great Commission. There is also the Great Commission, "Go . . . and make disciples of all nations" (Matt. 28:19). The Commission and the Commandment are two sides of the same coin, for love constrains us to share the gospel, and the gospel we share is a gospel of love, expressed in acts that reflect the love, mercy, justice, and righteousness of Jesus Christ. We are commanded and commissioned to serve as well as to proclaim. The gospel we preach and live is social as well as personal. It is a gospel of deeds as well as words. The gospel demands are directed to those who claim to have received it.

Five-minute Break   5 *(1:00)*

Exploring the Meaning of the Kingdom of God

EXERCISE 23: The Kingdom of God   *40 (1:40)*

Regather in the main circle and introduce the next topic as follows, or in similar words: "The central theme of the gospel Jesus preached and taught was the kingdom of God. The expression refers to the rule and the realm of God. It is important that we try to understand what is another paradoxical but powerful concept, and one that has been unfortunately neglected in the teachings of many churches."

Divide the participants into new groups of three or four, depending on the number in the class. Ask them to turn to Exercise 23 in the workbook, where they will find a list of forty-five biblical texts. Divide the list equally among the different groups and ask them to jot down in words, phrases, and succinct statements whatever insights they gain from their list of scripture passages. The groups can study the texts individually, then combine their research efforts. They should assign one person to record their findings on newsprint, to be shared later with the rest of the class. Allow plenty of time for this exercise.

Discussion. Regather in the center circle and develop a composite list as each group reports its findings, adding only what previous groups have not yet mentioned. Put the sheets on the wall for everyone to see. Paraphrase for clarity when necessary. Among other things they'll discover is that Matthew's Gospel uses "the kingdom of heaven" in all but three instances, whereas Mark and Luke use "the kingdom of God." The two expressions mean the same thing: "God ruling." John's Gospel has only two references to the kingdom of God. Paul and Peter refer also to the kingdom of Christ (Eph. 5:5; 2 Peter 1:11).

From *The Pastor as Evangelist* (pp. 50–51), read aloud the following excerpt:

> The parables of Jesus reveal the paradoxical nature of the kingdom, which is both present and future, realized and yet to come, fulfilled in Christ but not consummated, something God gives but which can be refused or missed. It is both the reign of God and the realm of God. The kingdom is God's,

not ours; God's to build and God's to give. Its signs are the words and works of Jesus, and to accept or reject Jesus is to accept or reject the kingdom.

If the message of evangelism has an appropriate kingdom emphasis it will be Trinitarian in its expression and church-related in its orientation. The fact that the kingdom is the rule of God is the basis and the thrust of the social gospel.

The message of evangelism, therefore, must include the good news of the kingdom, in the manner of him whom to know as Savior and to serve as Lord is the way to the kingdom, the truth of the kingdom, and the life in the kingdom.

Ask the class, "Why is the kingdom of God good news?" That should not be hard for them to answer, with the list on the wall in front of them, but it is good to give them a chance to verbalize their own understanding of the gospel of the kingdom of God.

Restating the Definition of Evangelism   5 (1:50)

Point out the New Age Dawning definition of evangelism, repeated on p. 14 of the workbook. Notice how it incorporates an emphasis on the kingdom of God. So too does the definition that follows, which is in effect a summary statement of the principles taught in this course, combining both the personal and the social dimensions of the gospel by calling people to personal faith in Christ and to obedient service in the world. There is also specific reference to the proclamation of the gospel in word and deed. Last, there is a third definition, which attempts to delineate a *style* of evangelism that is consistent with our Presbyterian emphasis on service. It is more a description than a definition.

Closing   10 (2:00)

Stand and sing a hymn or two. Then join hands around the circle for a "bidding" prayer. Invite people to share a need or a concern, a joy or a sorrow, or something or someone they would like the group to pray for or give thanks for. As a prayer request is mentioned, everyone present responds with a sentence prayer,

all praying aloud at once. The result is a chorus of voices all
praying to God on the same theme but each in different words.
Ask them not to mumble but to speak out, saying whatever the
Spirit lays upon their hearts to say. It is a very moving experience when all participate. When you wish to close, simply
suggest that the next request be the last; when all have finished
praying, offer a brief closing or benediction, or say something
like "Then all of God's people said . . ." and everyone else
responds, "Amen!"

WEEK NINE

Applying
the Gospel

Opening Devotions   *10 (10)*

Review   *5 (15)*

Make a brief summary statement: for example, "Having discussed the content of the gospel, including six different aspects and the central theme of the kingdom of God, now we are going to see how the good news applies to various social issues as well as to individual needs. The objectives for today's class are listed in the workbook." Ask someone to read them.

How to Apply the Gospel to Different People

EXERCISE 24: Applying the Gospel to Social Issues   *35 (50)*

Say, "The gospel is addressed to groups of people as well as to individuals, to nations as well as to persons, to systems and structures as well as to souls. In the light of all we have learned about the gospel, what is the relationship between evangelism and some of the problems and concerns of the world about us?"

Divide the class into groups of three or four, depending on the number of participants. Assign to each group *one or two* of the topics listed in Exercise 24 or some other contemporary issue, and ask the group members to see if they can agree on a brief Christian response to the question, based on their knowledge of scripture. One person should report for each group.

Discussion. Regather in the center circle and ask each of the groups to report on the issues they were studying. What conclusions did they reach? Invite comments from the rest of the class after each report before moving on to the next.

Ten-minute Break   *10 (1:00)*

EXERCISE 25: Applying the Gospel to Personal Needs *30 (1:30)*

The heart of all evangelism is one person telling another person about Jesus Christ, or, to use D. T. Niles's metaphor, "one beggar telling another beggar where to find bread."

Ask the participants to form the same small groups and turn to Exercise 25. Divide the questions among the groups and ask them to indicate their collective understanding of how the gospel would apply in each case. What aspect of the gospel might be most helpful or appropriate?

Discussion. After everyone returns to the center circle, go through the list one sentence at a time and have the reporter for each group read what they wrote. Ask the class to share their quick reactions to the different statements.

Visitation Evangelism

To introduce and describe service evangelism, ask the group to read "Service Evangelism" in the workbook. For ease of discussion you may prefer to read it aloud. Then, saying, "Our evangelism, we have seen, must be service oriented," go on to make the case for visitation evangelism.

The Case for Visitation Evangelism   *5 (1:50)*

From the example of Jesus we can derive several important principles to guide the evangelism of a particular church. As the class turns to "The Case for Visitation Evangelism," ask someone to read the four principles aloud.

The conclusion which follows logically from these principles is that a servant church will therefore have an organized and persistent calling program. This is the justification for what has been called, for want of a better term, "visitation evangelism." In view of the Great Commission and the Great Commandment, a church cannot ignore or shirk its duty to reach out to its neighbors in Christian love. Evangelism is not an option; it is a mandate from our Lord. With respect to visitation evangelism, the question is not *whether* to do it but *how.* It can be done with integrity and with a sensitivity that is winsome and appealing, because it is done by people who through service have earned the right to be heard. Ask the class if there are any questions.

Organizing for Visitation Evangelism

The subject of how to plan and implement an evangelism program for a local church is beyond the scope of this course. Pastors and church leaders who wish to pursue this topic further, however, will find an organizational outline for a visitation evangelism program, along with some suggested resources at the back of this guide.

Closing   *10 (2:00)*

You might introduce the closing devotional time something like this: "We have been doing some serious thinking together, and in the process I hope we have discovered, if we did not already know it, that it is indeed possible for Christians to differ in love. As a symbol of our love for each other and of our oneness in Christ, let's stand and sing 'We Are One in the Spirit'" (*WB* 619 or song sheet). Offer a closing prayer of thanks for the group and for the shared experience. Sing the benediction to the tune of "Edelweiss" (song sheet).

WEEK TEN

Developing Our Skills

Opening Devotions   *10 (10)*

Review   *10 (20)*

Take a few minutes to get some feedback on the home assignment. How did it go? Ask them to share some of their responses to Exercise 25. Comment that what they have been doing will be good preparation for interpersonal evangelism. Mention that you will be discussing the assigned articles, "Rules for Role Players" and "Guidelines for Role-Play Observers," and then have someone read the objectives for this week.

Evangelistic Calling Skills   *20 (40)*

Begin something like this: "Having made a case last week for evangelistic calling, it's time to learn how to do it. Some of you may be old hands at this, while for others it may be an entirely new experience. In either case, your task is to use your best communication skills, as you role-play different calling situations."

The Use of Role-playing. Many teachers of evangelism agree that the most effective method of teaching interpersonal evangelism skills (next to doing it for real) is role-playing. The effectiveness of the method, however, depends largely upon the cooperative spirit of the participants and the seriousness of purpose with which they enter into the experience. Your group has already done some role-playing during the course and should not be intimidated by it.

Rules for Role-playing. Ask the class to turn in the workbook to "Rules for Role Players," which was part of the home assignment. Role-playing can be a most instructive and constructive learning experience if the participants observe these four simple rules. As you read each of them again, ask if there are any questions.

When you have finished, divide the class into small groups. If there are fewer than eight persons in the course, you may want to do most of the role plays as demonstration enactments. If there are eight or more persons, divide them as equally as possible into groups of four or five. Five is the best number for role-playing most calling situations (two callers, two persons to be called upon, and an observer). Groups of four can function without an observer in situations that call for two calling on two, and at the end of the enactment they would evaluate themselves, with your help. If the situation requires only one person to be called on, the fourth person can be an observer. *The observation and evaluation at the end of each enactment is crucial to the learning process.*

Each role play is numbered and identified in the workbook, with a space provided for class members to write down what they learned. It is best to do this as they go along; otherwise, it can be done as part of the home assignment. Say that the groups will have up to fifteen minutes for each role-play enactment, followed by five minutes of evaluation. It is better to repeat the process as often as possible, rather than spending too much time on one role play. Since they will be calling two by two, one of the partners is to be the team leader and the other the support person. The leader should offer a brief prayer before they make their call—a *real* prayer, not part of the role play; pray *for* the role play, that it may be a worthwhile learning experience and that God will help them to practice what they have learned and to represent Christ and his church well. (If prayer is offered *within* the role-play situation, it is part of the enactment.) The callers are to act as they normally would unless told to do otherwise. The persons who are called upon are to act out the roles assigned them (consistency), unless they are moved by the situation to change (flexibility).

Guidelines for Role-Play Observers. These guidelines were also part of the home assignment. Be sure to underscore the importance of the observer. Ask if there are any questions about that role. Remind the class that the observer should be outside the conversational circle but close enough to hear and see what takes place. Most observers find it helpful to take notes. They do not merely repeat what happened but comment in a positive and constructive way on how well the callers listened, whether they missed any come-in points or plug-in points for faith-sharing, what the callers might have said or done differently, and so on. The people called on may respond to the observer's perceptions and share their own impressions of the visit, after which the callers may react to what has been said and share their feelings about what happened: Did we discover a need? Was it a faith-sharing experience (as defined on p. 15 of the workbook)? Should we have offered to pray before we left? and so on.

Suggestions for the Leader. After each role-play enactment, check to see how it went. Point out *briefly* any lessons to be learned from that particular situation, and be prepared to offer suggestions as to how they could best be handled. Your comments are extremely valuable in helping participants apply their interpersonal witnessing skills to the different situations, which are intended to give the callers experience in relating to all kinds of people in all kinds of circumstances.

To facilitate the shifting of roles and to enable you to give the same situation to all groups, work out a role-play rotation chart similar to the one on p. 72. It is most helpful if the groups have the same numbers of men and women with corresponding letters, so that when, for example you call the *C*'s and *D*'s aside to give them their respective roles, all the *C*'s are the same sex and all the *D*'s are the same sex. If not, you will have to be prepared quickly to vary the situations for the different groups according to the sex of those who are being called upon.

Role-Play Rotation Chart

Role	Role-playing Situations									
	1	2	3	4	5	6	7	8	9	10
Observer	A	B	C	D	E	A	B	C	D	E
Callers	B C	C D	D E	E A	A B	B D	C E	D A	E B	A C
Residents	D E	E A	A B	B C	C D	C E	D A	E B	A C	B D

Underlining indicates lead person.

Before each role-play enactment, take aside those who are acting as persons to be called upon (new residents, hospital patients, inactive members, next-door neighbors, etc.) and give them their roles. This can be done orally or in writing. Do not supply too many details. Leave room for their own imaginations to work. Use the suggested situation or make up one of your own. Give them a general idea of the kind of people they are to be. For example:

"Your name is Anderson. You are a grieving couple whose only child has recently died in an automobile accident. You have no church affiliation, and you are not too quick to open up, but you will do so if the callers are sensitive, caring people. One of you is very quiet; the other does most of the talking. The quiet one's body language gives a clue at some point of needing help, but doesn't volunteer the information. Let the callers draw it out by sensitive questioning. Try to enter into the situation and to feel the hurt of the persons you are playing."

The callers are told only what they would normally know or be told. For example:

"You are calling on the new residents of a home in your neighborhood. The name of the couple is Anderson, which information you obtained from a real estate listing. Your purpose, as always, is to offer your friendship, to express the desire of the church to be of service to the community and to them, and, if possible, to engage them in a faith-sharing conversation."

The observers may or may not be told the situation in

advance. There are advantages to doing it either way. If they already know the situation, they know what to look for and are more sensitive to the come-in points and plug-in points. If they know only what the callers know, they can evaluate the situation on the basis of their own perceptions. Usually the latter is more instructive for all concerned, but try it both ways.

You will continually be reminding all of the participants that how they make their Christian witness depends entirely on how the situation develops. *Trust the Holy Spirit!* This is not a canned approach. If we really believe in Jesus Christ, we know he wants us to do this, and we know the Holy Spirit will be with us in the enterprise. "Do not be anxious beforehand what you are to say; but say whatever is given you in that hour, for it is not you who speak, but the Holy Spirit" (Mark 13:11). What genuine Christian witness has not experienced the truth of Jesus' words over and over again? We can take heart in his promise to the disciples, who must have had the same fears we do: "The Counselor, the Holy Spirit, whom the Father will send in my name, he will teach you all things, and bring to your remembrance all that I have said to you" (John 14:26).

One or two of the participants may be a bit self-conscious at first, but they will soon get over it, when they discover how easy it is to become totally involved in the situation. Your own emphasis on the importance of this activity, which next to actual visitation is the best way to learn to do evangelistic calling, plus the prayers before the enactments and the comments of the observers, who take their role very seriously, all help to make it a most enjoyable as well as a worthwhile learning experience.

Tell the class that the calling process can be divided into different phases, such as the initial contact, getting started inside the home, the visit itself, and terminating the call. "We shall practice the first two phases and then put all the phases together, giving you a chance to use your newly acquired skills in a number of true-to-life situations. We'll begin with a demonstration enactment."

Role Play No. 1: The Initial Contact *20 (1:00)*

Calling Without an Appointment. In evangelistic calling it is not necessary to make an appointment in advance; indeed, it is impractical to do so, unless you want to make sure someone is home and can see you, before you make a long trip in vain. It is better for the callers to have a sufficient number of people to visit in a particular area and to take their chances on finding a percentage of those people at home. This rule applies especially to exploratory calls, where there has been no previous contact. It is too easy to say no on the telephone, especially to strangers. It's a different story, of course, if there has been some previous contact with the church. But if the church limits its callings to those who visit, the unchurched people in the community are never reached.

Callers who have not made an appointment in advance must acknowledge that fact right at the start and assure the residents that they will be brief. The sensitivity of the callers can compensate for the lack of an appointment. If the callers are never able to make contact, another approach is needed. Telephoning in advance requires some special skills, which we shall discuss later. For now we shall assume that no appointment has been made.

In visitation evangelism the first phase, or initial contact, takes place on the doorstep. It includes what happens before and what happens after you ring the doorbell. Ask for four volunteers. Two of them are to be residents; one of them is a caller along with you, the team leader; the fourth person is the observer. Set the stage as follows: "We are calling at a house the name of whose occupants we do not know. The lights are on, so it appears someone is home. My partner and I are part of the visitation evangelism program of Central Presbyterian Church."

Arrange a small circle of chairs to represent the living room of a house. Make sure the rest of the class can see and hear the enactment. The residents take their seats in the living room. The observer stands outside the circle and out of the line of vision. As leader you offer a brief prayer that what you are doing now may be useful to God and helpful to all. Knock on the door (the back of a chair will do). When the door is opened, say, "Good evening. I'm [name] and this is [name]; we're from Central Presbyterian Church, and we're calling on our neighbors. We know we're not expected, but could we visit with you for a moment? We promise not to stay long."

The response of the residents determines what happens next. You have deliberately not told them how to respond. They can decide spontaneously whether one or both of them will answer the door and how they will answer you. If they invite you in, fine; that ends the role play. If they talk with you at the door, fine; you continue your visit there. Sometimes, after a few minutes of conversation during which the resident has had a chance to size you up, you will be invited in. Under no circumstances should you try to talk your way inside; wait to be invited. If you are not admitted on the first visit, perhaps you or another team will get in the next time. If no one is home, write a brief note on a church bulletin saying you're sorry you missed them and you'll be back again another time. Leave it in the mailbox or under the door.

When you have ended the role play, give the observer a chance to comment, thank the other players, and then invite comments from the group. Point out that your purpose was to demonstrate the initial contact only. Your hope, of course, was that you would be invited to go in, but you did not want to be pushy.

The Opening Statement. Ask the class to turn to "What to Say at the Door" and have someone read the six things you expect to accomplish. If you know the resident's name, use it. Otherwise, say something like, "I'm sorry, but I don't know your name . . ." An expectant pause will normally induce the resident to tell you. Whether inside or on the doorstep, the caller is first a listener, showing interest in the other person and offering the friendship and service of the church in whatever way is helpful and acceptable.

Five-minute Break   5 *(1:05)*

Role Play No. 2   *10 (1:15)*

Having divided the class into groups of five (using color coding to expedite movement of larger classes), tell them that in the next role play *A* and *B* will be the residents, *C* and *D* the callers, and *E* the observer. *C* will be the leader this time and make the introductory statement at the door. Call the residents aside and tell them they are new to the community and their name is Jones. They are friendly but not inclined to admit strangers. Tell *C* and *D* that they are calling as part of the outreach ministry of First Presbyterian Church. In this case they know the name of the residents, having obtained it from a telephone directory which lists names and telephone numbers according to street address. Remind the callers to say a prayer before knocking on the door. Give them about five minutes for the enactment, then ask the observers to comment. During the role-play enactments it is helpful for the leader to move about the groups (being careful not to distract the participants) to assess their progress and help those who get off the track. After a few minutes, make any observations you wish.

Role Play No. 3   5 (1:20)

Switch roles according to the rotation chart. This time tell the residents to admit the callers. Once they're inside, the role play for this phase has ended. The observers comment and the players respond.

Role Play No. 4   5 (1:25)

Switch roles one more time. Tell the residents not to answer the door, as they are watching television and can't hear the knocking. The callers should leave a bulletin with a note indicating they will call again. Don't pound on the door! These three role plays are intended to give each of the participants a chance to play the role of a caller in this phase and to become used to and comfortable with praying before the call. The three situations are common occurrences.

Getting Started Inside the Home. "Once inside the house it is important that the situation be conducive to conversation. It is next to impossible to have a faith-sharing conversation when you are distracted by the TV, an overly friendly or unfriendly dog, attention-demanding children, lengthy telephone calls, subject-changing third parties, or loud-banging pipes.

"The callers should also try to avoid an unfavorable seating arrangement [see diagram on page 22]. If the situation can't be corrected, the callers would do better to make a graceful departure and come back another time. If the resident doesn't take the hint and turn off the television, it's obvious that he or she is not too interested in visiting. We're going to role-play some situations now to see how we would handle them. In each case we'll assume the callers have just been admitted."

The callers would normally begin by thanking the residents for inviting them in and by repeating their promise not to stay long. If they sense it is not convenient, even though they have been invited in, they should say something to that effect and offer to come back another time. Once seated they could start the conversation by restating the purpose of their visit: "We're calling on our neighbors to get acquainted and see if there is any way our church can be of service to them or to the community."

Role-playing Situations

Role Play No. 5 (demonstration) 5 *(1:35)*

Ask for three volunteers and demonstrate cross-firing, sidetracking, and yoo-hooing. What the callers should do to avoid a yoo-hooing situation is to ask politely if they could change their seats or move their chairs ("so we can hear you better"). If they find themselves in a cross-fire or sidetrack situation, they can say to the person who is engaging them, "Excuse me, I'm very interested in what you're saying, but I'm finding it difficult to concentrate with two conversations going at once." In order to get the point across, instruct the residents to be overly friendly and to talk fast and furiously and not let the callers get a word in edgewise, until the callers take charge. Take only two or three minutes to demonstrate each situation.

Role Play No. 6 5 *(1:40)*

Switch roles according to the rotation chart. Tell the residents (whose name is Riley) to make it obvious by their actions that the TV is on and they're watching a favorite show. They are coolly polite but keep glancing at the set. When the enactment is over and the observers have made their comments, ask the groups how they handled the situation.

Role Play No. 7   5 (1:45)

Switch roles. This time there is to be only one resident (Jackson). The other is an out-of-town guest who keeps changing the subject and monopolizing the conversation. See how the callers handle the situation.

Role Play No. 8 (if there's time)   5 (1:50)

Switch roles. Only one of the residents is in the living room this time; the other is in the kitchen. Their last name is Williams. The callers, having discovered that, can tactfully ask if the other person could join them.

Role Play No. 9 (if there's time)   5 (1:55)

Switch roles. Tell the residents, Sanchez by name, that they are Cuban, unchurched Roman Catholics, who are looking for a church in their new community. They want to talk about it and are very receptive. They speak English well.

Closing   5 (2:00)

Regather in the main circle for a brief closing prayer and benediction. Ask everyone to fill out Benchmark No. 3 from the back of their workbooks and turn it in to you before leaving.

WEEK ELEVEN

Building
Our Confidence

Opening Devotions *10 (10)*

Review *5 (15)*

You might begin with a brief statement such as this: "We have been practicing our interpersonal evangelism skills, and today we're going to see that these skills are applicable to any situation. As you continue your role-playing, I hope you are gaining confidence and competence as witnesses for Jesus Christ.

"The role-play situation at the end of the last class was a lead-in to what we're going to be doing now: role-playing the visit from start to finish—from the knock on the door to the departure.

"Remembering our call to be a servant church and our commitment to a service-oriented evangelism, we shall now role-play from start to finish some visits involving various situations that we encounter in everyday life. Unless an appointment has been made in advance, or there are some unusual circumstances to warrant a longer visit, an evangelistic call need not and should not exceed fifteen or twenty minutes, and neither should a role-play enactment.

"When it is time to leave, the callers terminate the conversation gracefully, thanking the residents for receiving them and concluding the visit in whatever way seems appropriate: an invitation? a prayer? a promise to return? an offer to do something? Was there a decide-to point? The callers' body language should be consistent with their verbal message at all times. If, for example, you say, 'We've interrupted you long enough; we ought to be going now,' look as if you mean it, by standing up as you say the words. If you are still slumping on the sofa, your body language is sending a different signal from your words. These are the kinds of things the observer should notice and comment upon. Remember, in every case the callers are hoping to engage the residents in a faith-sharing conversation, while being sensitive and responsive to any needs they discover. You are there to extend the hand of friendship in the name of Christ and to offer the services of the church in whatever way is needed and acceptable."

Role-playing Other Situations

Try to pick situations that allow you to do at least two and preferably three enactments in an hour. Use your imagination. Here are some possibilities; after the break, you may add situations brought to the class by the participants.

1. Someone of a different race or ethnic group (who doesn't fit into your homogeneous unit!). They wonder if they would be welcome.

2. A family of unchurched teenagers, who are somewhat militant and antagonistic. They are rock music fans and are experimenting with drugs. Their parents are divorced and the young people are living with their mother, who works at night as a waitress.

3. A single elderly person too infirm to live alone, who ought to be in a nursing home but doesn't realize it—and can't do anything about it anyway.

4. A young couple who are presently unchurched but are thinking about "getting back to church," now that they are expecting a child.

5. Inactive members who are angry at the church for all kinds of reasons, but whose real problem is that they are out of work and financially strapped and resent the church's stewardship appeal.

6. New residents who were active Presbyterians in their former community and are eager to transfer their membership to a church in their present community.

7. Young people who are on the rolls but have been inactive

ever since they joined the church as ninth-graders. Their parents, who attend church occasionally, are not at home when the callers arrive.

8. Members of another denomination who are presently unchurched.

9. Friendly adherents of another religion, who are delighted to engage in a faith-sharing conversation.

10. Militant agnostics who want to argue about religion but who have no answers for the death of their daughter.

11. A single person who has visited your church a few times but has never thought of joining and has never been baptized.

You would want to add a few descriptive details to each of these situations, but not too many. Give just enough detail for the residents to know how to proceed, but allow them to develop their own characterizations of the types of person they are playing. Usually some need will surface with sensitive listening on the part of the callers. Sometimes the need is obvious and acknowledged, sometimes it is hidden. But there is almost always a come-in point for a caring caller.

Role Play No. 10 *25 (40)*

Divide the class into new groups of five. Using the rotation chart, call the residents aside and give them a situation to role-play, drawing upon your combined awareness of real-life situations. Life is stranger than fiction! Don't make the first situation too difficult, however. Let it be one in which the residents have a discoverable need and are receptive to the caring approach of the callers. See if the callers discover the need and if they are able to engage in a faith-sharing conversation. Was it God-centered? Was it Christ-centered? Did they invite a faith decision? Did they pray at the end? If they didn't, should they have offered to? What is the next step? These are the kinds of things about which the observers comment. After the groups have evaluated themselves, you can raise some of these questions, to make sure the observers are carrying out their function correctly. Tell the role players you will give them about 15 minutes for the enactment, at the end of which you will give a signal for them to make their graceful exit. Then they will have 5 minutes for a debriefing. Allow about 25 minutes altogether, including your preliminary instructions and brief comments at the end. Point out the importance of how they terminate the visit and make their departure.

Role Play No. 11   25 (1:05)

Try to spend no more than 25 minutes on any one enactment; some can be done in much less time, depending on the situation. If a conversation does take place, you would usually want to give the players about 15 minutes, as in the previous enactment.

Five-minute Break   5 (1:10)

Before breaking, ask the class to turn in their written descriptions of faith-sharing situations, and choose from among them some which you feel would be especially good to role-play. When you use one of theirs, be sure to call attention to that fact. It underscores the relevance of the training experience.

Role Play No. 12   15 (1:25)

After the break, switch roles again. Use one of the participants' situations. Set the stage according to their written description. Signal them when to end their visit. Find out how it went. What were the pitfalls? What did they learn? What did they do right? What should they have done that they didn't do? In the case of the residents who were unchurched members of another denomination, for example, the callers should refer them to the nearest church of that denomination, but check back a few weeks later to see if the situation has changed.

Role Play No. 13   15 (1:40)

Switch roles and give them another situation. A wide variety of situations will give the participants a chance to practice their interpersonal witnessing skills under differing circumstances. You can also slip in a few extenuating circumstances now and then to help them remember about handling distractions and dealing with the unexpected.

Role Play No. 14 (if there's time)   *15 (1:55)*

Switch roles and go through the process again with a totally different situation.

Note: If you would like to vary the teaching approach, you could make use of some of the training films and videocassettes that are available. The participants can view and comment on the films. Instead of a role-playing enactment, you could allow the participants to "brainstorm" about some situation in which they have been called upon to share their faith. To facilitate the process, it would be best to divide into threes, so that there would be time for each person to present a situation for discussion within the group. You might also suggest that members of the class could get together at their mutual convenience sometime during the week to role-play some of the situations that there is not enough time to include during the class session.

Closing   *5 (2:00)*

Regather in the center circle. Ask, "How are you doing? Are you feeling more confident about your ability to do the work of an evangelist? What have you learned about yourselves? What have you discovered about faith-sharing? Any other comments?" After a time of sharing, close with a brief prayer.

WEEK TWELVE

Putting It All Together

Opening Devotions   *10 (10)*

You may want to plan a special devotional exercise to begin this final class meeting.

Review   *5 (15)*

Call attention to today's objectives. Introduce them by saying something like this: "We have been focusing on home visitation because it is the core of a church's evangelistic outreach to the community. But our interpersonal witnessing skills are not limited to evangelistic calling. In addition to evangelistic calls, we can role-play other situations in which we are given an opportunity or can create an opportunity to engage others in a faith-sharing conversation."

Here are some possibilities, to which you can add many of your own ideas.

1. Two deacons are delivering flowers to a member in the hospital. The patient in the other bed of the semiprivate room is desperately ill.

2. A conversation on the "nineteenth hole" of the golf course among a foursome, two of whom are secularists who would say they believe but don't show it in any way.

3. A conversation between two couples at a P.T.A. meeting. Their children are friends, but one family is unchurched and the child is getting no spiritual training whatsoever.

4. Two high school students at a party are trying to persuade

a third to smoke marijuana with them. The third youth has recently joined a church on confession of faith.

5. Two stewardship callers encounter a family who are neither attending nor supporting the church in any way.

6. Office employees are chatting during their lunch break. The witness is asked by the other three why she or he believes in "all that religious stuff." They scoff at the church.

7. Your Jewish neighbors want to know what right you Presbyterians have to try to proselytize people of other faiths.

8. One of the children in your Sunday school class asks, "How do you know there's a God?" The other children want to know too.

9. Your employers' treatment of one of your co-workers is unfair and inhumane. You feel obligated to confront your employer on behalf of your colleague. You happen to know that your employer is a Presbyterian. You are standing, while your employer sits behind a desk.

10. Church members are entertaining prospective members at home, seated at your dinner table. They have visited the church, but have never joined any church. They are friendly.

Role-playing Situations Outside the Home

Role Play No. 15   *20 (35)*

Assign the participants to new groups. Give them a situation to role-play from the above list or one suggested by the participants. After they debrief, make whatever comments you feel would be helpful and then move on to the next enactment.

Role Play No. 16   *10 (45)*

Switch roles and continue with the next situation. Make this a quick one, such as a hospital call to deliver flowers, or a short exchange at the checkout counter of a supermarket.

Role Play No. 17   *15 (1:00)*

If there's still time before the break, switch roles and do

another totally different enactment, using one of the participants' suggestions or one from the above list. Remind the class to jot down each situation and what was learned in each role play in their notebooks under the appropriate role-play number.

Five-minute Break 5 *(1:05)*

Using the Telephone

The final three role plays involve telephone calls. You might say something like this: "The telephone can be used effectively when there has been previous contact with the person being called, or when there would be obvious interest on the other person's part in hearing from the church. It is not a good medium, however, for initiating contact with strangers. Nothing can substitute for a personal visit.

"If you feel it is necessary or helpful to telphone in advance for an appointment to visit inactive members or those who have visited your church, the steps to take are given in the workbook under 'How to Use the Telephone.' Further thoughts on using the telephone are given in the other reading assignment for today, 'Three Rules for Telephone Callers.'"

Role Play No. 18 *10 (1:15)*

Use triads for this enactment. Set the stage this way: *A* and *B* sit back to back. *A* telephones *B* for an appointment, after *B* has attended church a couple of times as a visitor. *B* is resistant but not unreasonable; if *A* uses good interpersonal communication skills, *B* will respond positively and agree to an appointment. *C* observes *A*'s introduction, statement of purpose, and listening skills. Was the purpose clearly stated and a definite time, date, and length of meeting agreed to? How was the closure? Allow about five minutes for the call and five for the debriefing.

Role Play No. 19 *10 (1:25)*

Switch roles and repeat the exercise, suggesting a different situation.

Role Play No. 20   *10 (1:35)*

Switch roles and repeat the exercise. This allows each person to take each part. Suggest a different set of circumstances for this call.

A Brief Review   *10 (1:45)*

Regather in the center circle. Summarize what has been covered in the course, using the goals for each week as the basis of your review. Then talk about the second part of the course. Explain to the participants what is involved in the supervised calling experience: They will meet one night a week for the next four weeks to make assigned calls in the neighborhood. Ask them to indicate which of the scheduled times they will be available. Debriefing after the visits will follow the same style of the debriefing of the role plays. A system for record-keeping and follow-up will have to be established, and much thought given to the entire assimilation process.

Sharing Reactions   *10 (1:55)*

After dealing with any questions, refer to the composite list of "hopes" that the class compiled at the beginning of the course. Put the sheets back up on the wall for all to see and go down the list one by one, asking various members of the class to respond. "In what ways have your hopes been realized or not realized?" Give them time to express what the experience has meant to them, to affirm one another, and to recommit themselves by God's grace to being "Christ's faithful witnesses to their life's end."

Closing   *5 (2:00)*

That's a good lead-in to a final brief devotional exercise, which you and members of the class should plan in advance. At the conclusion, thank them again for their faithful attendance and participation throughout Part One of the course, and ask them to fill out and turn in their evaluation sheets before they leave. Also remind them that Part Two, the supervised calling experience, begins next week (announce the day and time). "We've been gearing up for twelve weeks. Now we put into practice what we've learned."

The harvest is still plentiful; let's rejoice that there are now a few more laborers!

Organizing for Visitation Evangelism

While it is essential in communicating the gospel for churches to adopt methods of evangelism that are relevant for all levels and conditions of contemporary society, there is no substitute for the personal witness of one individual to another. A sports program, a coffeehouse, or a street-corner ministry may be effective ways to reach certain groups of people, but there is only one way to reach everyone in the community, and that is through a thorough and persistent program of visitation evangelism.

This is an appeal for every particular church to take seriously its mission within its own neighborhood and its responsibility to minister to the community of which it is a part. To do that the church will need to define the geographical boundaries of its parish, determined not by where the members live but where the church serves.

The goal of the church's evangelism is not merely to increase the membership, although this will follow as a natural consequence of such an effort. The goal is rather to be faithful to our calling as servants of the Lord Jesus Christ, who ministered to people's needs. In the name of Christ the church reaches out to people through a systematic program of door-to-door calling, in an effort to reach every home in its parish.

In some instances a call may amount to no more than a friendly invitation to come and worship, or to participate in some aspect of the church's life and work. In others it will be an opportunity for personal witness and a sharing of faith at whatever level the situation calls for. In every case, it will be an effort to encourage those who are unchurched to come into the fellowship of a local congregation. Whether or not they do, the church will offer its services and make itself available in whatever ways are appropriate and acceptable.

Every local church should be mission-minded and evangelistically sensitive. Evangelism is not a program that a church adopts for a time; rather, it is part of the mission of the church to be evangelistic. Visitation evangelism is simply the procedure through which a church carries out its mission to the community and expresses its evangelistic concern.

It is the Christian education function of the church to help those who are brought into the church to grow in their faith and understanding and to express their faith in appropriate and meaningful action in the church, the local community, and beyond.

There are many ways to organize for visitation evangelism, and each presbytery, through its committee responsible for evangelism, stands ready to encourage and assist its member churches in their task. It is hoped that churches will take advantage of the Evangelism Consultant Service. Contact your local presbytery office for information on how to engage a consultant. The outline below suggests some procedures which have been effective in some churches and which can serve to stimulate other ideas that may be more easily applied to a given situation.

What the Presbytery Can Do

There are many things the Presbytery Committee on Evangelism can do to help the churches of the presbytery do the work of an evangelist. They include the following:

See that one or more persons are trained to serve as Evangelism Consultants for the presbytery.

Invite representatives of a church with an effective evangelism program to share their experience with the committee.

Search out members who are qualified to speak knowledgeably on the subject and who would be available to meet with particular church committees interested in organizing for visitation evangelism.

Let churches know by letter and by announcements at presbytery meetings that help is available.

Present periodic reports at presbytery meetings, using examples of particular churches that have had successful programs of visitation evangelism.

Gather, develop, and make available to local congregations various resource materials, including books, pamphlets, training films, and filmstrips.

Subscribe to and make available to churches a cross-reference telephone directory which is organized by street addresses instead of people's names, such as those published by Cole Publications.

Sponsor various kinds of evangelism events, including conferences, seminars, workshops, and especially this Presbyterian Evangelism Training Course, taking advantage of the many resource persons and programs available.

Organizing the Particular Church

The particular church is where the action is. But there is not likely to be any evangelistic action without the leadership and support of the pastor and the session. If they are committed to an evangelistic outreach, it will happen. If they are not, it will not.

So the first requirement is a commitment on the part of the pastor to the need for visitation evangelism in his or her own parish. The pastor must realize that there are unchurched people out there who need to hear the gospel of Jesus Christ and who could benefit from the ministry of a caring congregation. There is a missionary frontier in the church's own back yard.

When the pastor is convinced of this, he or she will share the vision with the session and enlist support in planning and organizing for evangelism, including a visitation program. In most churches the responsibility for planning and supervising the church's evangelistic ministry should be delegated to an evangelism committee, which ought to be either a standing committee of session or a subcommittee of a standing committee.

The Calling Program

It should be clearly understood that the evangelism committee exists not to do the church's evangelistic work but to enlist and equip the whole church for its evangelistic ministry. The committee's task is primarily organizational, motivational, educational, and promotional. The members of the committee ought not be perceived by the rest of the congregation as the church's semi-professional evangelists. Rather, they are catalysts for congregational evangelism.

The outline that follows lists the essential steps.

I. PRELIMINARY WORK

   A. Enlistment of Volunteer Workers
      1. Recruiters: to contact people by phone or in person to enlist callers
      2. Officer helpers: for such things as record keeping, summary reports, street address lists
      3. Kitchen crew: to provide refreshments for callers
      4. Callers: for exploratory calls, follow-up calls, challenge calls
      5. Baby-sitters: to enable persons with small children to participate

   B. Publicity (to encourage participation)
      1. Personal invitation (the best way!)
      2. Church bulletin notices
      3. Pulpit and church school announcements
      4. Telephone calls and letters
      5. Posters and flyers
      6. Word of mouth (enthusiastic support of the program)

   C. Preparing the Congregation
      1. Sermon series relating to faith and faith-sharing, the

mission of the church, evangelism, and witnessing
2. Small-group meetings to inform, inspire, and motivate
3. Person-to-person sharing of the need for evangelism
4. Letters from the pastor and the session sharing their vision of and commitment to evangelism and urging the congregation's involvement, support, and prayers
5. Stressing the theme "There is something everyone can do!"

D. Involving the Congregation
1. Constantly suggesting ways for people to be involved and supportive
2. Helping people to discover their gifts and see how they can help the church's ministry of evangelism
3. Encouraging people to use their gifts to help the church evangelize
4. Continually reminding members to bring friends and neighbors to church
5. Undergirding the entire ministry with prayer (corporate and private, pastoral and congregational, intercessory prayer groups and individuals)

E. Designing Forms for Record Keeping
1. Survey cards: to obtain information about families in the neighborhood
2. Follow-up cards: to show results of each call
3. Street lists: block-by-block master lists of all residents
4. Prospect list: kept chronologically for recall and cross-reference
5. Prospect list: kept alphabetically for recall and cross-reference
6. Prospect file: alphabetical file of all prospect cards

F. Strategic Aids
1. Cross-reference or reverse-street telephone directory (sometimes called a "crisscross directory"), an invaluable aid in identifying residents by address
2. Voter registration lists: another aid in identifying residents by address
3. Real estate listings: an aid to spotting changes of property ownership in the neighborhood

4. Attendance registration cards or pads: signed by worship attenders
5. Church guest book: signed by some visitors

G. Training Materials
   1. This Presbyterian evangelism course, *Faithful Witnesses*
   2. Pamphlets on evangelism: Good News Booklets, New Age Dawning materials and evangelism and general information
   3. Pamphlets on witnessing: from your presbytery committee or evangelism consultant; better yet, develop your own!
   4. Pamphlets on calling: available with specific suggestions on how to make an evangelistic call
   5. Bibliography: see Resources for Visitation Evangelism in the back of this guide (your church library or the pastor's library should have a number of these reference books on various aspects of evangelism; encourage people to read them)

H. Calling Materials
   1. "How to Join the Church": Develop your own flyer describing the process to prospective members
   2. Church folder (with updatable inserts): These describe the church's current ministry and program and are also useful in stewardship calling
   3. Church bulletin: The best calling card, with its various announcements, church calendar, and order of service, the bulletin is a picture of what's going on; callers can leave a written message on it, when no one is home
   4. Church newsletter (copies of the church's weekly or monthly newsletter or other publication, if any)
   5. Other specialized literature (such as flyers announcing coming events)

II. THE CALLING PROGRAM

A. Essential Principles
   1. It must be well organized or it won't be effective.

2. It must be top priority or it won't be supported.
3. It must be consistent or it won't be sustained.

B. A Definite Time
1. The same season of the year: Choose the season best for your area (many prefer calling in spring and fall, on a three-months-on, three-months-off basis).
2. The same day or night each week: Choose your own, but stick to it!
3. The same time each day or night; it should not be too late or too long: Start and end on time, probably about 7:30 to 9:00 P.M. for evening calling, plus another half hour for reporting and debriefing.

C. A Definite Place
1. An appropriate meeting room: It should be large enough and comfortable.
2. Space priority for the program: The callers should not be shunted from room to room every time some other group wants to use their meeting place.
3. Access to the kitchen (if there is one): Refreshments enhance the fellowship during discussion times.

D. One Suggested Format (adjust to suit your circumstances)
1. 7:15 P.M.: Briefing. Callers report for briefing and assignments. The pastor or the evangelism chairperson assigns the calling teams and distributes the cards, giving any specific instructions or information that might prove helpful. Newcomers are teamed with experienced callers.
2. 7:28 P.M.: Prayer. Ask God to prepare the way and bless the callers in their witness. Remind the callers to have a word of prayer with their teammates before and after each call.
3. 7:30 P.M.: Callers depart in teams of two. Callers are instructed not to ring any doorbells after 9:00 P.M. and to return to the church as soon after that as possible.
4. 9:00 P.M. Callers return. Information on each call is reported on the card, dated, and initialed by the callers.

5. 9:10 P.M.: Discussion. Serve light refreshments as the teams report, sharing and reflecting upon their experiences and offering comments to one another. This is part of the ongoing training and can be an extremely valuable learning experience for all.

6. 9:30 P.M.: Closing prayer. Thank God for redeeming and using the efforts of the callers and ask God's continued blessing on those who have been visited, and who may be wrestling with a decision of faith or struggling with personal problems.

E. Sources of Prospects

1. Exploratory calls: There are many more unchurched persons in most communities than some churches realize. Reaching these people is evangelism in its truest form. As the visitors reach out in an ever-widening circle with the church at the center, more and more unchurched persons will be discovered, many of whom may not be the least bit receptive at first. To reach some of them may take years of persistent calling, caring concern, and prayer. But they are well worth the effort! Any unchurched person is a potential member if not a prospective one. How long do they remain on the prospect list? Until they join your church or some other church, move out of the community, or die!

2. Neighbors, friends, schoolmates, and relatives of church members

3. Unchurched co-workers and colleagues of members

4. People who have attended worship services and signed a pew card or a church attendance registration pad

5. People who have attended weddings, funerals, baptisms, or other special services

6. People who have attended special activities or programs at the church

7. Unchurched parents of children in the Sunday church school

8. Unchurched members of the choir or some other organization in the church

9. People who have used the pastoral services of the church (such as counseling, funerals, weddings)
10. Parents of children in the nursery, day care center, or weekday or vacation Bible school
11. Referrals from other churches or religious organizations
12. Unchurched young people in the youth group
13. Unchurched persons met through casual encounters
14. Members of organizations that use the church facilities
15. New residents in the community
16. Friends and family of those who have been married, baptized, or buried at the church

F. Types of Calls

Evangelistic calls can be divided into different types. Some callers are more comfortable with a particular type of call.

1. Exploratory calls: on families or individuals where there has been no previous contact, to discover if the individuals are unchurched and if there is any kind of need in which the church can be of service
2. Follow-up calls: on families or individuals who have been visited before and who have been discovered to be unchurched
3. Calls on inactive members: to learn the reason for the inactivity and see, again, if there are not unmet needs to be filled
4. Challenge calls: on the militant agnostics or atheists who appear to want to argue about religion (these calls are made as time permits, by the most capable callers)

G. Assigning the Calls

1. The cards of those to be called on each time are selected after much prayerful consideration by the pastor and the evangelism chairperson, who continually peruse the earlier callers' comments, to see when a particular follow-up call should be made
2. Cards are arranged geographically in packs of six to twenty each, depending on the type of call (survey calls take less time)

3. Whenever possible, make card assignments in advance; at least some advance work can be done in assigning cards to those who have indicated they would be calling at a given time

H. Categorizing Prospective Church Members
When a church engages in visitation evangelism it will find itself with a growing list of names of prospective church members. For purposes of record keeping and especially in reviewing cards for possible follow-up, it is important to have some system for classifying and filing these cards, even though any such system will be admittedly quite arbitrary and subjective. In every case the card will indicate any special needs that the church should address or help address. It is expected that a church will have established an adequate support system to deal with the kinds of human needs a service-minded evangelism inevitably reveals. The names of such persons are then referred to the appropriate organization, agency, group, or individual for whatever service or follow-through is needed. The categorization system relates, of course, not to needs, which vary and fluctuate, but to the persons' status with respect to church membership. Since each church has its own nomenclature for classifying prospects, the following letter categories are offered only as a suggestion:
A cards: Persons who have said "Send for my letter of transfer" or have indicated they wish to join on reaffirmation or profession of faith and are attending or have committed themselves to attend a series of membership preparation classes
B cards: Persons who have indicated interest by attending services and other church activities but have not yet committed themselves to join
C cards: All unchurched persons, regardless of the reason, and those whose membership is in an out-of-town church, one too far away for them to attend (this is the basic category, from which it is hoped that a person will move through B to A)

D cards: Persons who have not yet been called upon and whose religious affiliation is not yet known; exploratory calls have yet to be made

E cards: Persons who have indicated an affiliation with or a preference for another denomination but who have not yet joined a church in the community (these are referred to the nearest church of their professed denomination, and a follow-up call is made within a few weeks to see if contact has been made)

F cards: Some churches find it helpful to have a separate category for self-declared atheists, militant agnostics, and nonbelievers; these are the so-called "challenge" calls, which require more time and much prayer. Not every caller is equipped for or committed to this kind of challenge. Never underestimate the transforming power of the Holy Spirit, who will use and reward your patience and persistence in wonderful and surprising ways!

I. Reporting Results
   1. Callers' reports of their visits should be briefly and legibly recorded on the card, dated, and initialed
   2. Pertinent information and the callers' recommendation regarding future action should be included
   3. The current prospect category is indicated by letter at the top of the card and changed as the person's situation changes
   4. The oral account given during the reporting time can amplify the information on the card

J. On-the-Job Training During the Oral Reporting
   5. The callers share their experiences and suggest to each other ways of increasing their effectiveness as witnesses
   6. The pastor or evangelism leader comments on ways various situations were handled
   7. The meaning, purpose, and methods of evangelism are reviewed from time to time

K. Referral of Needs
   1. Shut-ins, the elderly, the sick, and others who may need special attention are referred to the Board of Deacons or some other appropriate organization or group within the church
   2. Those needing pastoral services are referred to the pastor or someone trained for such calls
   3. Those with needs that exceed the capacity of the church to respond are referred to the appropriate social agency or service organization within the community, or to whatever organization or group can best deal with the particular problem, need, or concern; in these cases the church functions as the catalyst for action
   4. This kind of service-oriented evangelism requires a commitment to ministry and a willingness to sacrifice on the part of the particular church, which must be a faithful corporate steward of all its resources in its effort to meet the needs of people

L. Related Things to Do
   1. Have a regular attendance registration at worship, explaining to the congregation why it is important
   2. Have a series of orientation classes for prospective members, climaxed by a meaningful service of reception, to give integrity to the process of joining the church
   3. Enlist church members to serve as sponsors or "special friends" of new members and to shepherd them through the assimilation period
   4. Involve new members *meaningfully* in the fellowship and work of the church
   5. Sensitize all of the church organizations regarding their evangelistic responsibilities and opportunities
   6. Establish training programs to equip church officers, leaders, teachers, and members to share their faith with confidence and integrity
   7. Continue to train and equip those who are serving as visitation evangelists

Resources for Visitation Evangelism

Allan, Tom. *The Face of My Parish*. New York: Harper & Brothers, 1957. Out of print but available in theological seminary libraries.

Armstrong, Richard Stoll. *The Oak Lane Story*. Division of Evangelism, United Presbyterian Church U.S.A., 1971. Out of print but available in many seminary and church libraries.

————. *Service Evangelism*. Philadelphia: Westminster Press, 1979. See especially chapters 6, 9, and 10.

Conning, Keith, and Mae Fern. *The Brookwood Story*. Published privately, 1985, by Keith Conning, 2472 East Livingston Avenue, Bexley, OH 43209.

Eakin, Mary M. *Scruffy Sandals: A Guide for Church Visitation in the Community*. New York: Pilgrim Press, 1982.

Johnson, Ben. *An Evangelism Primer: Practical Principles for Congregations*. Atlanta: John Knox Press, 1983.

Kennedy, D. James. *Evangelism Explosion*. Wheaton, Ill: Tyndale House, 1970.

McPhee, Arthur G. *Friendship Evangelism: The Caring Way to Share Your Faith*. Grand Rapids: Zondervan Publishing House, 1978.

Sweazey, George E. *Effective Evangelism*. Rev. ed. New York: Harper & Row, 1976.

————. *The Church as Evangelist*. New York: Harper & Row, 1978.

Tucker, Grayson L., Jr. *Person-to Person Evangelism*. A Good News booklet. Evangelism Program, United Presbyterian Church U.S.A., 1981.

Visitation Evangelism: A Relational Ministry and *Visitation Evangelism: A Guide for Laity,* VHS videotape cassettes produced at Louisville Presbyterian Theological Seminary, 1982.

Other Books on Evangelism

Arias, Mortimer. *Announcing the Reign of God: Evangelism and the Subversive Memory of Jesus.* Philadelphia: Fortress Press, 1984.

Armstrong, Richard Stoll. *The Pastor as Evangelist.* Philadelphia: Westminster Press, 1984.

Hendrick, John R. *Opening the Door of Faith.* Atlanta: John Knox Press, 1977.

Hunter, George G. III. *The Contagious Congregation: Frontiers in Evangelism and Church Growth.* Nashville: Abingdon Press, 1979.

Johnson, Ben Campbell. *Rethinking Evangelism: A Theological Approach.* Philadelphia: Westminster Press, 1987.

Mission and Evangelism: An Ecumenical Affirmation: A Study Guide for Congregations. New York: Division of Overseas Ministries, National Council of Churches, May 1983.

Padilla, C. René. *Mission Between the Times: Essays by E. René Padilla.* Grand Rapids: Wm. B. Eerdmans Publishing Co., 1985.

Articles, Booklets, and Other Resources
(from New Age Dawning bibliography)

"Affirm the Good News," adopted by the 189th General Assembly of the United Presbyterian Church in the U.S.A., 1977, and presented to the 118th General Assembly of the Presbyterian Church in the United States, 1978.

"Channels of God's Love and Power" by Leon Wright and Grady Allison.

"Church Growth Guidelines," by Frank A. Beattie, Jr., and John F. Haberlin.

"Congregational Evangelism Checklist" prepared by Frank Beattie.

"Directions for Mission" approved by the General Assembly

Mission Council of the United Presbyterian Church in the U.S.A., in 1972.

A *Manual for Year Round Evangelism in the Local Church* ed. William F. Emery. Revised 1983.

"One Mission Under God," paper of the 119th General Assembly of the Presbyterian Church in the United States, 1979.

"Response to God's Saving Grace: Evangelism and Peacemaking" by Richard Killmer.

"The Theological Basis for Evangelism," statement of the Presbyterian Church in the United States, 1976.

"Toward a Reformed Theology of Church Growth" by Paul Fries.

"Workshop Model for Managing Fears About Evangelism" prepared by Frank Beattie.

Good News Evangelism Booklets. Order from Evangelism Program, 1101-P Interchurch Center, 475 Riverside Drive, New York, NY 10115.

New Age Dawning materials published by the Evangelism Program of the Presbyterian Church (U.S.A.), including Presbyterian Evangelism Consultants materials.